P536: MAKING SCHOOL-CENTRED **INSET** WORK

P536:
Making School-centred INSET Work

THE OPEN UNIVERSITY
A SCHOOL OF EDUCATION PACK FOR TEACHERS

PATRICK EASEN

THE OPEN UNIVERSITY
in association with
CROOM HELM
London • New York • Sydney

© 1985 The Open University
Croom Helm Ltd, Provident House, Burrell Row,
Beckenham, Kent, BR3 1AT
Croom Helm Australia, 44-50 Waterloo Road,
North Ryde, 2113, New South Wales
The Open University, Walton Hall, Milton Keynes MK7 6AA
Reprinted 1986 and 1987

British Library Cataloguing in Publication Data

Easen, Patrick
    Making school-centred INSET work: a School
    of Education pack for teachers. — (P536)
    1. Curriculum planning — Great Britain
    I. Title. II. Open University
    575'.001'0941 LB1564.G7

    ISBN 0-7099-1945-X

Published in the USA by
Croom Helm
in association with Methuen, Inc.
29 West 35th Street
New York, NY 10001

Library of Congress Cataloging-in-Publication Data

Easen, Patrick.
P536. making school-centred INSET work.

    Bibliography: p.
    1. Teachers — In-service training — Great Britain.
2. Curriculum planning — Great Britain. I. Title.
LB1731.E15 1985   371.1'46'0941   84-23078
ISBN 0-7099-1945-X

Typeset by Columns, Reading
Printed and bound in Great Britain
by Billing & Sons Limited, Worcester.

CONTENTS

What is This Book About?   ix
How Might This Book Help You?   xiii
A School of Education Pack from the Open University   xv
Acknowledgements   xvii

Section One: Introducing School-centred INSET   1

1 Coping With the Challenges of School Life   3

The Way Things are in Schools   3
Arguing about the Curriculum   4
Teaching is about Survival   5
The Myth of the Hero-innovator   6
Perceiving the Culture of School-centred INSET   7
Using These Materials   9
Organising Yourself and the Work   12
Using This Approach for the First Time   13
From Here on   15

2 Curriculum Change, Co-operation and Conflict   16

Exploring Mutual Professional Problems   16
Considering the Conflict Which may Arise   17
Reflecting Upon the Nature of Conflict in Real Life   19
Finding Ways of Resolving Conflict   20

Section Two: Changing the Curriculum   23

About This Section   25

3 Exploring School Issues   27

The Difficulty of Beginning   27
Shared Concerns   28
Shared Experience   29

4 Considering the Problem   30

The Importance of Problem Formulation   30
Considering Constraints   31
Considering Appropriateness   33
Brainstorming   33

Classifying   35
Making the Problem Manageable   36
Before Moving on   36

5 *Tackling the Components of the Problem*   38

Thinking of Ideas for Resolving the Problem   38
Building on the Brainstorming   38
Raising Questions   40
Preparing to Collect Information   41
Checking with Colleagues   42

6 *Collecting Information*   43

Sources of Information and Their Use   43
The Need for Flexibility   43
Classroom Observation   46
Analysing Classroom Observations   48
Joint Classroom Observations   50
Visits to Other Classrooms and to Other Schools   51
External Expertise   53
Being Prepared to Re-frame the Problem   54

7 *Establishing a Successful Resolution*   55

Murphy's Warning   55
Deciding on Appropriateness   56
Into Action   57
Final Thoughts   59

Section Three: Change and You   61

About This Section   63

8 *Professional Learning*   67

What Does Learning Involve?   67
What Really Makes an Impact?   71
When Professional Learning Means Personal Change   72

9 *Personal Learning*   73

Learning about Ourselves   73
The Complexity of Ourselves   73
The Social Construction of Ourselves   77
Confronting Ourselves   80
From Knowledge to Action   82

10 Transforming Professional Realities   84

  Being Practical   84
  Self-appraisal   84
  Controlling Your Experience   86
  Other People Can Help You   86

Section Four: Change and Others   89

About This Section   91

11 Handling Denial   93

  The Discomfort That Leads to Denial   93
  Games as a Substitute for Communication   95
  Confronting Denial   96
  New Rules for Old Games   98

12 Resolving Conflict   99

  From the General to the Particular   99
  Reviewing Your Own Perception of the Conflict   99
  Using a 'Third Party'   100
  Resolving Through Re-framing   101

13 Supporting Change   103

  The Conundrum of Professional Learning   103
  Invitations to Change   104
  The Need for Help and Support   106
  Approaches to Support   106
  Support through Communication   107

14 Improving Communication   108

  Communication for Growth   108
  Constructive Feedback   109
  Self-disclosure   110
  Getting the Message   111

15 Learning through Discussion   112

  Making Discussions Work for You   112
  A Basic Difficulty of Group Discussions   113
  Characteristics of Good and Bad Discussions   114
  A Structured Approach to Discussion   115
  Overcoming Difficulties of Discussion   117
  Beyond Discussions   118
[This chapter is based on ideas developed by Graham Gibbs and Andrew Northedge in the Open University's Institute of Educational Technology]

16 Working in Groups   119

  Group Life   119
  Making Your Group More Effective   119
  Coping with the Practicalities   122
  The Fundamental Need for Trust   122

Section Five: Overview   125

About This Section   127

17 Sustaining the Approach   129

  The Challenge for School-centred INSET   129
  The Processes of Effective School-centred INSET   130
  Institutionalising the Processes   132
  The Power of Teachers   135
  In Conclusion   137

Section Six: Guide to the Activities   139

About This Section   141

18 Focus of Each Activity   143
19 Types and Times of Activities   147

Section Seven: Appendices   151

    I. The Saber-tooth Curriculum   153
   II. The Myth of the Hero-innovator and Alternative
       Strategies for Organisational Change   161
  III. Fundamental Activity for Every Group Meeting   169
   IV. 'Scoring Points'   171
    V. 'Victor'   175
   VI. 'The Year the Schools Began Teaching the Telephone
       Directory'   178
  VII. Cartoon   184
 VIII. 'Arithmetic'   185
   IX. Games Educators Play   186
    X. Confronting Avoidance   188
   XI. 'The Three Year Itch'   191
  XII. 'A Fuzzytale'   194

Bibliography   197

WHAT IS THIS BOOK ABOUT?

This book has been written against a background of increasing emphasis upon an approach to in-service training for teachers (INSET) described by Rudduck (1981) as 'school-centred', i.e. an approach embracing,

> both 'school-based' activity, a mode of in-service education which takes place on the school premises, and 'school-focused' activity, a mode which accepts that the professional requirements of the school and the staff as a whole provide a focal point around which a whole programme of in-service work is planned.

The premise being that, because school-centred INSET is more immediate, then it is likely to be more effective. Certainly, the very real problems confronting individuals and groups of teachers within any school are affected by factors specific to that school as well as by more general factors. Logically, then, any resolution of such problems has to evolve within that web of specific factors. The approach itself, however, raises a number of questions and practical difficulties for those at the chalk-face.

This book is intended to provide practical guidance and support for *any* teachers who wish to work together in their schools in order to review and develop their pupils' experience of the curriculum. It will also be useful for those who are expected to fulfil a 'leadership' or 'consultancy' function in relation to the curriculum. It is a very flexible book and enables you to work at your own pace on your own content, taking account of school priorities rather than any 'study' or 'course' priorities.

Our starting point is that there is – and will continue to be – increasing pressure upon schools and teachers for greater accountability. These pressures emanate from many quarters both within the education service, such as the Department of Education and Science (DES), Her Majesty's Inspectors (HMI) and Local Education Authorities (LEA), and beyond it, such as parents, media and society in general. A public service consuming public money, it is felt, should be available for public scrutiny and public comment. Gone are the days of the 'secret garden' of the curriculum. At the same time, most teaching decisions are independent ones, made in solitude, behind closed classroom doors. Often such decisions are made in haste and under pressure, but the school, and the professionals in it, will be held responsible for the consequences of those decisions. This book sets out to help teachers ensure that the quality of those decisions is the best possible in the circumstances.

You will find that most of the work falls into three sections, each of which focuses on an important aspect of school-centred curriculum development, describing some of the component strands within that aspect and suggesting activities to support practical work in that area.

Change and the Curriculum deals with the theme of mutual problem-solving by groups. It is intended to help you and your colleagues explore issues concerning the life of your school, formulate these as problems, and systematically collect information to resolve these problems.

Change and You deals with the reciprocal relationship between the behaviour of the school as an organisation and the behaviour of an individual within it. It is intended to help you consider how pressure for change impinges upon an individual and ways of coping with it.

Change and Others deals with the theme of relationships between those within the school. It is intended to help you and colleagues improve communication, develop mutual support and operate as an effective group.

As with most Open University materials, P536 was produced by a group of people whom we call the 'course team'. They were:

Patrick Easen: Course Team Chairperson and author of the print materials

Lizzie Dawtrey: Course Team Co-ordinator and academic responsible for developing the video material

Elaine Brown: Course Team member

Sally Clay: Course Team Secretary, responsible for ensuring that talk was translated into action!

Meg Sheffield: Course Team member, BBC Producer, responsible for the video material

Hossein Zand: Course Team member, responsible for co-ordinating and evaluating feedback

In addition, the course team has benefited from regular contact and discussion with the *external assessor* for the Pack, Dr Christopher Day, Director of the In-Service Unit, University of Nottingham.

We also must acknowledge that, without the help and support of Ellison Platt, Project Controller of the Open University, these materials would never have got off the ground. The ideas and the materials themselves have been developed with, and tried out by, teachers in Buckinghamshire, Bedfordshire, Clwyd, Devon, Grampian, London, Oxfordshire and Sheffield.

Throughout the production period the Course Team had invaluable advice and comments from many other people. These included other members of the Open University, members of other institutions and, in particular, teachers who were prepared to carry out work in schools on our behalf.

We would like to take this opportunity of expressing our sincere gratitude to all who have helped in the design, production and criticism of the P536 materials.

HOW MIGHT THIS BOOK HELP YOU?

Teaching seems to defy precise analysis. Since, in so many ways, it is an area of uncertain knowledge, when engaged in it or thinking about it we often draw strongly on metaphors. A skilled teacher at work makes continuous selections from within his or her repertoire of experience, knowledge and techniques to achieve results. Each teaching and learning situation is unique, and the accomplished teacher uses that selection not as a rule to be applied, but as a possible metaphor for examining the situation. The unfamiliar, unique situation is seen by the teacher as both similar to and different from the familiar one, without at first being able to say similar or different with respect to what. In doing this a teacher has to rely in part on intuition – reason alone is not enough.

Teaching is also the type of activity which tends to engender a feeling of isolation as we face the countless instant decisions we are required to make in the course of a day. Often we have to respond to difficult situations by relying on our own intuition without pause for thought, and yet at the same time any teacher is responsible to the pupils, the parents, the school, the governors and the local authority for the consequence of any one of those decisions. On top of the demands of teaching itself are the demands of professionality, the pressure to review frequently what we are doing as we teach.

No wonder that feelings of pressure, confusion, frustration or isolation are commonplace among teachers. This book cannot solve those particular problems for you. What it can do is to offer some very practical ways for you to handle issues of curriculum review and development within your own school and, in doing so, possibly contribute to your solving of the other problems for yourself. In particular, the activities try to do this by building on what already exists, although often it is only in an implicit form. For example, many teachers tend to have fairly regular conversations with one other person, either another teacher on the staff or a friend. This is an important way of deriving some support for their work even though that may be an unspoken, or even unconsidered, part of the relationship. So in the book it is both *stated* that such support should be used, and a *structure* provided in order to facilitate it. In other words, we make explicit recognition of relationships involving support.

The aim of this book is to help you, in co-operation with your colleagues, to review and develop the curriculum actually experienced by the pupils in your school. We hope that, through using these materials, you will:

(1) *Increase your understanding* of your own feelings, thoughts and actions in relation to your activity as a teacher within your school.

(2) *Develop your repertoire of choices* for handling both the educational experience provided for the pupils in your school and your relationships with your colleagues.

(3) *Try out for yourself* some of these new ways of handling your professional life.

(4) *Make decisions* about what 'works' and makes sense in relation to your particular school.

The stumbling blocks to school-centred INSET – and the professional learning it involves – are indeed many. In this book we attempt to help you to identify and surmount some of them. We hope that our suggested activities will integrate with whatever work you are already doing. The purpose of the first section is to introduce you to the approach, outlining the main themes covered in the materials, and suggesting how you might make the ideas come alive for you.

A SCHOOL OF EDUCATION PACK FROM THE OPEN UNIVERSITY

This book has been written as part of a set of Open University materials called *P536: Making School-centred INSET Work*. It is a pack, not a course, so there are no OU tutors, no assignments and no set study programme. You can study it where and when you like, and work through whichever bits of the materials you choose. To give you a rough idea of how much work is involved we have provided an estimate of times required for particular activities. You can find these estimates in Section Six, Guide to the Activities pp. 147-9.

This book forms the core of the set of P536 materials. The other materials available are:

(1) A sixty-minute video cassette with video notes which has been especially made for the P536 pack and provides a view of one school's experience of school-centred INSET. It is not attempting to show 'good practice', but a specific set of responses provided by real teachers and improvised by them for the cameras. Printed notes are included with the video. These provide a synopsis of the video and some suggestions for its use in schools.

(2) 'A Guide for Group Leaders' is a book designed for anyone who wishes to stimulate and support school-centred INSET e.g. an LEA adviser, a Teachers' Centre Leader or a lecturer in Higher or Further Education. It contains suggestions and further activities for an organised eight-session course on the subject. Such a course, for example, might be arranged for subject co-ordinators in primary schools, subject heads of department in secondary schools or members of school management teams.

If you want more details of these items, or would like to provide feedback on your own experience of using the P536 materials, please write to:

P536 Course Manager
The School of Education
The Open University
Walton Hall
Milton Keynes
MK7 6AA

ACKNOWLEDGEMENTS

The publishers gratefully acknowledge permission from the following to reproduce copyright material: Punch Publications Ltd, London, for the illustrations on pp. 1, 89, 108; Mike Turner, Brentwood, Essex, for the illustration on p. 23; John Morland, Ramsey, Isle of Man, for the illustration on p. 61; Universal Press Syndicate, New York, for the Ziggy cartoon on p. 84; Kenneth Mahood, London, for the illustration on p. 94; Councils and Education Press Ltd, Longman Group, Harlow, Essex, for the illustrations on pp. 67, 104; BBC Publications Ltd, London, for the illustration on p. 125; McGraw-Hill Book Co., New York, for the illustration on p. 154; Nigel Paige, London, for the illustration on p.184.

Appendix I is from *The Saber-tooth Curriculum* by J. Abner Peddiwell, courtesy of McGraw-Hill Book Co., New York. Appendix II is from *Behaviour Modification with the Severely Retarded*, Kiernan and Woodford (eds.), courtesy of Elsevier Science Publishers B.V., Amsterdam. Appendix V is from *Thunder and Lightnings* by Jan Mark, courtesy of Penguin Books Ltd, London. Appendix VI is from *The Year the Schools Began Teaching the Telephone Directory* by Merrill Harmin and Sidney B. Simon, courtesy of *Harvard Education Review*. Appendix VIII is from *Arithmetic* by Carl Sandburg, courtesy of Granada Publishing Ltd, London. Appendix XI is from *The Three Year Itch* by Angela Anning, courtesy of Times Newpapers Ltd, London. Appendix XII is from *A Fuzzytale* by Claude M. Steiner, courtesy of Grove Press Inc., New York.

SECTION ONE
INTRODUCING SCHOOL-CENTRED INSET

"I see you adopting a more rational approach to problem-solving."

1 COPING WITH THE CHALLENGES OF SCHOOL LIFE

The Way Things are in Schools

Any attempt to review or tackle curriculum issues within a school is, by definition, to put the *status quo* within that school under a microscope. What goes on in the daily life of any school is the result of many different things. Just describing the warp and weft of school life is usually difficult; explaining it is almost impossible. It is, however, the way things are in the school for all the participants, teachers and pupils; it is represented by a vast array of routines and habits and constitutes the actual curriculum of that school.

We all tend to be creatures of habit and rely on it considerably as we live out our lives. Most of the time the routines of our practice are not called into question; for a start, we are often too busy to bother.

Staffrooms are an important part of the daily life of the teacher

Sometimes, though, any attempt to examine – and perhaps change – what goes on implies that the activities and the social relations making up that delicate *status quo* are brought to the surface. Sometimes, too, that *status quo* represents conflicts at truce; truces negotiated, possibly unconsciously, over a period of time and enshrined in the way individuals relate to each other. In turn, these social relations and their accompanying behaviours will be part and parcel of the way those involved think. So it is that any disturbance can lead to personal or collective stress. When that happens people may react in any number of ways, thereby shattering those unspoken truces.

Within our staffrooms we all tend to play certain 'games', and in particular when it comes to change. We play them for a number of reasons: to avoid self-confrontation, to conceal ulterior motives, to justify current behaviour (and therefore avoid changing it) or simply to avoid participation. Such things can seriously impair our ability to act together to tackle corporate problems.

When people have to work together and co-exist, they often leap-frog over scores of differences and potential difficulties that can come back to haunt them. Curriculum review and development can present an arena in which this may happen. When that happens, arguing about the curriculum can be the cloak for a host of other arguments. These, then, are the nerve endings of school-centred INSET, the conflicts, overt or covert, that can come to exist within organisations and, without the resolution of which, good intentions will come to little.

Arguing about the Curriculum

Activity 1: tackle individually

An extract from 'The Saber-tooth Curriculum' is reproduced as Appendix I, pp. 153-60.

(1) Read the extract.
(2) Consider whether you have ever experienced a curriculum 'debate' comparable in some way to this story.

In 'The Saber-tooth Curriculum' the defendants of the original curriculum (consisting of fish-grabbing, woolly-horse-clubbing and saber-tooth-tiger-scaring) argue against those seeking to change the curriculum to net-making, antelope-snaring and bear-killing. It is, of course, satire, and as Swift reminded us, 'Satire is a sort of glass, wherein beholders do generally discover everybody's face but their own.' We all know that reality is far more complex than any models that we can construct for thinking about a situation. On the other hand, a model, even a satirical one, can help us to concentrate on what seem to be the essentials of the real situation, filtering out some aspects but emphasising others. So it is that we can laugh at the way those involved in 'The Saber-tooth Curriculum' perceive the situation as a conflict of interest, missing the opportunity to explore really the fundamental issue involved. When it comes to reviewing our own curriculum, however, are we in danger of treading the same path?

Teaching is about Survival

Although teaching involves very high-level and complex skills it is essentially a practical art rather than an intellectual process. It draws on our ordinary practical knowledge, and often requires us to 'think on our feet'; in other words, to think about doing something while doing it. Becoming a teacher is a demanding experience and, at least in the early days of being a probationary teacher, is concerned with learning how to survive and how to cope in a classroom.

Being involved in the act of teaching means having to cope daily with the masses of information with which any teacher is faced. Becoming 'experienced' involves learning what to look for and how to respond to what we find. In order to do this we have to filter out some things so that we can deal with the rest. When we stop to examine this intuitive

We all develop our own ways of handling everyday teaching situations

filtering, this sorting out of the wheat from the chaff, we see that we have, in effect, developed a theory of our own for handling everyday situations – what might be called a 'theory of action'. We may not be able to describe this theory to anyone else – not, that is, without considerable reflection and analysis. Indeed, much of our teaching behaviour may be at an intuitive and implicit level, but we do build up this implicit set of rules as a result of our learning, each day, to handle classroom problems as they arise. This is the basis of our 'survival kit'.

If we want to change our curriculum this will affect our personal 'theories of action'. In fact, this is probably what makes curriculum change difficult. If our own theories are deeply buried they may be very difficult to change – they may be very powerful, but very resistant. Perhaps we should make a habit of bringing them up to the surface from time to time – if only to see if we still agree with them! So if we wish to make changes we often have to begin by confronting ourselves, and in order to do this we need to reflect on our own behaviour or practice, make explicit the theories buried in that practice and critically examine them. This in itself is difficult enough to do when *we* want to do it. When we feel pressured by someone else to do it, our professional life may threaten to become intolerable.

The Myth of the Hero-innovator

As teaching requires each of us to make so many decisions every day in the solitude of our own classrooms, it is also a very personal type of work. Our lives and personalities become inextricably bound to the work we do. For this very reason we may wish to influence and change the work of others; and for the same reason we may resent the efforts of others to change us. Most of us have had experience of the educational crusader. The phenomenon is referred to by Georgiades and Phillimore (1975) as 'the myth of the hero-innovator', i.e. 'A knight in shining armour who, loins girded with new technology and beliefs, will assault his organisational fortress and institute changes in himself and others at a stroke.'

Many a sharp innovative sword, however, has been blunted on the strong shields of survival kits. As Georgiades and Phillimore point out, 'organisations such as schools . . . will, like dragons, eat hero-innovators for breakfast'. The net result is often little more than a feeling of disillusionment on the part of the hero-innovator and feelings of resentment or frustration on the part of his or her colleagues. Rarely does the school benefit from the experience.

"To you it may be just a windmill but to me it's The System!"

Activity 2: tackle individually

The article 'The Myth of the Hero-innovator and Alternative Strategies for Organisational Change' is reproduced as Appendix II, pp. 161-7.

(1) Read the first section of the paper, pp. 161-3.
(2) Consider how this description compares with your own experience of attempts at educational change.

The effectiveness of any attempt to change the practice of an organisation such as a school has less to do with its structure (which can be precisely described and, indeed, changed) than with its culture (which is very difficult to analyse and describe).

Perceiving the Culture of School-centred INSET

Activity 3: tackle individually

---

(1) Run your fingers over the table-top or arm of the chair (or whatever) where you are working now.
(2) Jot down what you feel.

When asked to do that activity, very few people jot down 'the compression of my fingertips' (or something similar). Usually the answer describes some quality of whatever has been touched. Yet it is only through the differential compression of our fingertips that we can feel the surface and appreciate the qualities of things. We perceive *from* the compression of our fingertips *to* the qualities we explicitly acknowledge. What we tend to do is make tacit that immediate perception (of compressed fingertips). If we did not do that it might get in the way of our perception of the ordinary world.

So it is with curriculum change. We tend to focus our attention on the superstructure of curriculum change and fail to perceive the foundations upon which that is built. Tucked away in the corners of our professional minds is knowledge which we use to help us engage in professional activity with our pupils and with our colleagues. It is the type of knowledge that we get access to by doing, like, for example, riding a bicycle, but which we do not, or cannot, easily articulate. The trouble is that 'tucked away' is often where the knowledge stays, unrecognised and therefore not consciously used. The approach of this book is based on the belief that, by making explicit the knowledge which is implicit, you and your colleagues may generate some ground rules for effective school-centred curriculum development. Any curriculum change has a personal dimension for *each* teacher involved and an institutional dimension created by the interactions of *all* of those involved. Attempts to tackle a curriculum issue, as a school-based level, needs an interplay between the three elements:

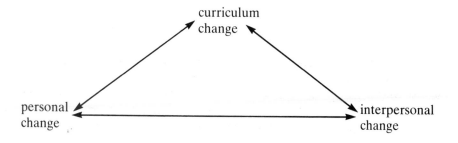

Although *curriculum change* may be concerned with the process of identifying, defining and resolving problems specific to a particular school, often any real change implies:

● *personal change* as we often need new ways of looking at things if we are really to change what we do; and
● *interpersonal change* to encourage effective communication so that any necessary support can be sought and given during the process of change.

In these materials we try to encourage you to consider each of these dimensions.

Using These Materials

(1) GROUP MEETINGS The materials are only part of our approach. *The most important element is the basic format that we recommend for every meeting of your curriculum group.*
We suggest that each meeting consists of three stages:

(a) *Working on your particular curriculum issue or problem.* This is the *content* of your school-centred INSET, and is determined by your own priorities in your own school. For example, the focus of the meeting might be to examine the effects of parental pressure upon the teaching of mathematics. It should take the majority of the time set aside for any meeting, for example 1 hour in a 90-minute session.

This content should be *negotiated*, with everyone having to state explicitly – not just be given the opportunity to state – what they see as the purpose of the meeting. Once each participant has considered and contributed his/her own view, the group can move on to determine what should be done and how. This may, on occasions, take quite a long time; on other occasions it will be dealt with very quickly since it may require no more than the confirmation of what had been tentatively agreed at the end of the previous meeting. The steps at this stage of the meeting might be:

● each participant considers and contributes his/her own answer to the question: 'What do I want to get from this meeting?'
● the whole group negotiates an agreed goal by answering the question: 'What can we agree to act upon as a group?'
● the whole group identifies alternative courses of action by answering the question: 'What are the alternative ways of doing this available to us?'
● the whole group makes a commitment by answering the question: 'What shall we actually do?'

(b) *Reflecting upon the process of working on your particular curriculum issue or problem.* This concerns the *process* of school-centred curriculum development as experienced by you and your colleagues. It requires you to reflect upon your action and that of your colleagues during the first part of the meeting. A crucial way to discover more about how you function – and why you are sometimes successful at one thing and sometimes a failure at something else – is to examine what you are actually feeling at the time you are engaged in doing something. Thinking about what has happened, and its significance for you, helps you to generate 'personal knowledge'. It is this type of knowledge that you will find useful for future activity because, having created it, you will also be able to apply it.

This stage of 'reflection-in-action' is vital for your learning. In a 90-minute session at least 20 minutes should be devoted to it. After reflection you will find it helpful to write down in a fairly structured way what you have been thinking and doing; this enables you to reflect upon your reflections before sharing them with your colleagues.

Writing down what you have been thinking and doing helps you reflect

This writing is often the hardest for people to do, but they do find it surprisingly helpful and powerful. The steps at this stage of the meeting might be:

● each participant considers and contributes his/her answer to the question: 'Can I give two examples of where we worked well together?'
● each participant considers and contributes his/her answer to the question: 'Can I give two examples which lead me to think that we can improve our performance?'
● each participant considers and contributes his/her answer to the question: 'What have I learnt about school-centred curriculum development today?'

The group should not comment upon anyone's contribution at this stage, merely listen to each person in turn.

(c) *Negotiating and deciding future activity.* This helps you to consider what you now might do in the light of your experience of both the content and the process of this meeting. You may, for example, decide each to carry out classroom observations to collect information related to your curriculum issue. On the other hand, you may decide that the group discussion had not been as productive as it might have been and that the group would benefit from considering this further. The point is to try to establish some agreement as to what you, as a group, will do next time you meet, and what you each might do in between the meetings to facilitate the work. It is at this stage that you may decide to draw upon some part of these materials as the basis for what you plan to do; for example, the session 'Classroom Observation' in 'Changing the Curriculum' or 'Learning through Discussion' in 'Change and Others'. Try to keep this stage brief, about 10 minutes at the end of your 90-minute session, but if members of the group want more time to think about it try pinning up a notice for suggestions in the staffroom.

The step at this stage of the meeting being:

● the group considers and decides the answer to the question: 'What action can we take to improve what we are doing?'

In diagram form, your group meeting will be like this:

Stage One: Working on the agreed curriculum issue
Stage Two: Reflecting on Stage One
Stage Three: Deciding what to do next

A summary of this section can be found in Appendix III, pp. 169-70; do refer to it at each group meeting.

(2) THE MATERIALS Access to and use of any section of this book is controlled by you and your colleagues. There is no set sequence or interrelationship between the materials other than that we anticipate you reading Section 1 first. Each of the main sections of this book corresponds to one of the dimensions of school-centred INSET mentioned earlier:

Curriculum Change $\longrightarrow$ Section 2: 'Changing the Curriculum'
Personal Change $\longrightarrow$ Section 3: 'Change and You'
Interpersonal Change $\longrightarrow$ Section 4: 'Change and Others'

A list of the main themes for each section can be found in the table of contents, and a detailed index to activities can be found in Section 6, 'Guide to the Activities', pp. 139-46. You should use these to help inform your decision-making.

(3) PRIVATE WORK As a result of both the group meetings and use of the materials, you will be required to *do* things and *think* about things. Often this consists of writing down your thoughts and experiences and talking through things with one or two other people, either before or during a group meeting. Sometimes this may seem either too trivial or unnecessary to do (or both), *but do persevere since it provides a structure for a dialogue with yourself that encourages a deeper exploration of the real issues and problems*. Our experience from the development work has been that committing thoughts and feelings to paper has been found to be extremely useful. We recommend that you keep a work-folder with two sections: one for any notes relating to the work done with your colleagues on the curriculum issues, the other section consisting solely of a diary of your responses to stage (b) of the group meetings ('Reflecting upon the process of working on your particular curriculum issue or problem').

The 'P536 approach' with the group meetings, use of materials and private work, may appear unusual. However, it is really quite simple and straightforward and you should soon get used to it. Like most simple things, however, it takes skill and effort to get it right and make it really work for you. *You may also find that you feel resistance within yourself to doing some of the activities or completing the work. Don't worry; real learning can be risky and stressful at times. If you start to experience such feelings try jotting down what you are feeling and why.*

Organising Yourself and the Work

This book is based on the belief that real curriculum development results from professionals tackling mutual problems in a participative manner. Nevertheless, there will be a certain amount of organisational matters needing to be sorted out – someone needs to act as chairperson, circulate notes or whatever. 'Leadership' is a rather overworked concept, particularly in relation to the curriculum, you will not need to be 'led', but you will need to be organised. Much of this you can do for yourself; some things relating to the group may need to be delegated or rotated. This issue of organising yourself or being organised by others is tricky. Some people almost insist on being passive and indeed submissive. Unfortunately, we have only ourselves to blame. Education often insists on taking more and more responsibility for learning away from the learner, creating, in the process, a self-concept of dependency. Dependence enables us to attribute successes and failures to others without acknowledging our own responsibility and power. *Each person using the P536 pack should accept responsibility for his/her own learning, and one way of doing this is to organise himself or herself as much as possible during the work.*

Using This Approach for the First Time

Negotiation and reflection are key features of the P536 approach to school-centred INSET. It may seem slow and possibly daunting, but it does seem to work. Experience suggests that most people are over ambitious when first embarking upon school-centred curriculum review and development. *It is usually more fruitful to begin with something contained and small scale.* For example, rather than trying to carry out a thorough review of the mathematics teaching in the school, it would be better to start by considering, say, the mistakes that pupils often make in computational work and ways of handling them. Once you and your colleagues have taken a sliver of your practice and successfully reflected upon it, you will be in a stronger position to move on to some other aspect of your practice.

A school which is able not only to engage in the practice of educating its pupils but also to reflect systematically upon that practice might be termed a 'thinking school'. Achieving a 'thinking school' in which the process of curriculum review and development is institutionalised is a long-term goal. This approach will help you to move towards it, but, in the first instance, *be wary of organising yourselves for a longer time-scale than one term.* This provides 'containable' time which helps you determine your objective for the work; in itself a crucial thing because, as a result of using these materials, you ought to have a tangible outcome at the end of that time.

It is almost impossible to generalise about where to begin. It really does depend upon the particular circumstances of each school. *Clearly the momentum for your work should come from your agreed curriculum issue* and part of the group's function is to determine which activities of this book will support and further the work. Getting started, however, is difficult, and will require you to consider a number of factors such as who is involved, what the group is hoping to achieve, the time available and so on. Some possible options to consider for the first meeting might be:

(1) *If* it is to be a 'fun session' and also engender discussion about how the group can work together, *then* try starting with activities 4, 5 and 6 in Chapter 2.

(2) *If* the group needs to agree on a possible curriculum issue, *then* try starting with activities 9 and 10 or 11 and 12 in Chapter 3.

(3) *If* the group already knows what curriculum issue it wants to tackle, *then* try starting with activity 13 in Chapter 4.

(4) *If* the group wants to examine the 'theories of action' buried in the classroom practice they 'know', before deciding on an issue, *then* try starting with activity 22 in Chapter 6.

(5) *If* the group wants to get a 'feel' for the nature of the activities in this book and their demands, *then* try starting with activities 70, 71, 72 and 73 in Chapter 15.

Option (1), of course, might be a 'stimulating' way of starting the ball rolling before then trying options (2), (3) or (4) – the possible permutations are endless.

Do remember to check the estimated times of activities beforehand so that you can decide what needs to be done before the meeting and what can be done there – and don't forget stages (b) and (c) of the meetings format! Attempts to involve whole school staffs in school-centred INSET have often met with only limited success. Often people expect too much too quickly. In a sense, that is irrelevant for you at this stage. The important point is that you may be studying these materials with just a few of your colleagues and feel that others should be involved. Does this matter? Only you can answer that question. It *may* be that the issue concerned is genuinely not relevant to all members of staff. For example, it may only affect one department in a secondary school or a particular age-range in a primary school. Even if that is the case, whatever actions you take as a result of the work may have implications for other members of staff. On the other hand, the issue may be one which is not only of concern to other members of staff but requires their active co-operation for the effective implementation of any action. *Whether it is a question of not being appropriate for some groups or individuals to become involved, or they choose not to do so, it would be unwise not to build bridges to those people.* Some ways of doing this are by:

(1) Ensuring that the actions and decisions of those involved are communicated and understood . . . including getting feedback.

(2) Continually seeking ways of working effectively with others.
(3) Anticipating and eliminating any potential 'boundary' or responsibility problems before they arise.
(4) Really trying to listen to others and doing all that is possible to help them listen to you.

Perhaps others may find that they want to join in later, that possibility should be open to them.

From Here on

Pressure for change can be like a Pandora's Box, bringing stress, tension and even conflict in its wake. In Chapter 2 we consider some practical ways of achieving a supportive climate in which the rest of the work might then flourish. You may decide to base your first meeting on activities 4, 5 and 6 in Chapter 2. If not, do keep the ideas in mind. After the first meeting use the rest of the materials as suggested on pp. 11-12. These materials are not intended to produce a neatly packaged course. Although your work on it may have an obvious beginning, you may find it less easy to define a 'middle' or an 'end'. In Section 5 you will find an 'Overview'. This is intended to help you step back from the experience and see just what it has meant for you. It will not, however, 'tie up loose ends', rather it will help you and your colleagues to produce a 'position statement' of yourselves for yourselves. The thing is that these materials are the beginning, not the whole, of a way of making school-centred INSET work in your context. Do make them work for you in achieving that aim.

2 CURRICULUM CHANGE, CO-OPERATION AND CONFLICT

Exploring Mutual Professional Problems

The approach underpinning this book is not about the process of persuasion, that is getting other people to do, say or think what we want them to do, say or think. Neither is it about a definitive management style for education. It is about exploring mutual professional problems with colleagues.

Coercion and manipulation are inappropriate in this whole area of curriculum review and development. When we coerce someone we usually know for certain that we are in the right, and therefore ignore the ideas or views that the other person may have. After all, these are either irrelevant or strategies for delay! In order to do this, however, we need to have a suitably large 'stick' which is recognised as such by the victim. On the other hand, manipulation still sees the other person's views as a nuisance. However, instead of ignoring them we subvert them by twisting their ideas to our own purpose. This may well imply some form of 'carrot'. Neither 'sticks' nor 'carrots' are relevant to this approach.

The situations which concern us most as teachers often have certain features; the most striking ones being:

● it is not always easy to make sense of all the information confronting us in a particular situation;
● some of the most important situations we want to deal with are unique in that we have never experienced anything quite like it before;
● often the difficulty is not solving the problem but knowing what the problem is in the first place;
● there are no fixed, clear and given ends, instead they are uncertain, obscure, ambiguous and conflicting.

In conditions such as these we may have perspectives but we do not have certainties. Even if we did, we could never really get our own way for, at best, we can only ever be indirectly (rather than directly) responsible for the transactions between another teacher and his or her pupils. What we can do is respect the ideas and views of the other person without necessarily agreeing with them. Success, then, is not measured by the complete acceptance by the other person of one's own view, but by the increase of willingness and ability to work together in a touchy situation or to solve a tricky problem.

The way we think about each other, the way we talk with and at each other and the way we behave with each other are vital to the success of school-centred INSET. All of us, at some time, feel surrounded by people who appear to be going out of their way to misunderstand us or thwart our intentions. It is too easy to blame other people in such situations – in fact much easier than stopping to consider how effectively we were getting through to each other in the first place.

Considering the Conflict Which may Arise

Often, conflict is seen as something caused by certain people and, by definition, something which can be avoided. It is, however, more realistic, to accept that it is an inevitable and integral part of the process of change. Not only this, a certain amount of conflict is a necessary and useful part of the life of any group; it prevents complacency and stimulates new thinking. Indeed, Irving Janis (1977) coined the term 'Groupthink' to describe errors of decision-making based on group conformity. The symptoms of 'Groupthink' being:

(1) an illusion of invulnerability, shared by most or all of the members, which creates excessive optimism and encourages taking extreme risks;
(2) collective efforts to rationalise in order to discount warnings which might lead the members to reconsider their assumptions before they recommit themselves to their past policy decisions;
(3) an unquestioned belief in the group's inherent morality, inclining the members to ignore the ethical or moral consequences of their decisions;
(4) stereotyped views of rivals and enemies as too evil to warrant genuine attempts to negotiate, or as too weak or stupid to counter whatever risky attempts are made to defeat their purpose;
(5) direct pressure on any member who expresses strong arguments against any of the group's stereotypes, illusions, or commitments, making clear that such dissent is contrary to what is expected of all loyal members;
(6) self-censorship of deviations from the apparent group consensus, reflecting each member's inclination to minimise to themself the importance of their doubts and counter-arguments;
(7) a shared illusion of unanimity, partly resulting from this self-censorship and augmented by the false assumption that silence implies consent;
(8) the emergence of self-appointed 'mindguards' – members who protect

the group from adverse information that might shatter their shared complacency about the effectiveness and morality of their decisions.

Conflict, however, has two sides. When it is constructive, people can exchange different views about a problem and it encourages new ideas. When it is destructive, it undermines what people are trying to do *and* the people who are trying to do it. We all recognise destructive conflict, it is characterised by:

- individuals perceiving their 'image' as being threatened;
- personalities intruding;
- conflicts being expected, resulting in a self-fulfilling prophecy;
- people arguing about different things without realising it.

Of course, we all like to think that what *we* do is underpinned by rational argument; that *we* are open to new evidence and that, because of this, *we* are capable of modifying and improving our views. If this is true then all conflict would be constructive. Perhaps, *if* we can articulate our beliefs and are clear about how these concepts are formed, *then* we can proceed in a fairly rational and constructive manner. The trouble is that often we aren't very good at articulating the theories implicit in our actions. Instead, because our beliefs are ingrained in our being and we value them for the help they give us for being effective in the world, we feel under threat and pressure. Instead of looking hard at any inadequacies in our ways of making sense of the world, we become ever more defensive of them.

Activity 4: tackle as a group

This activity is based upon a game called 'Scoring Points'. It is both fun to play and insightful. If you have attended a course based on P536: 'Making School-centred INSET Work' you may have played 'Win as much as you can', and providing you have sufficient players, you may prefer to play 'Win as much as you can' as an alternative to 'Scoring Points'.

(1) Read the instructions for 'Scoring Points', Appendix IV, pp. 171-4.
(2) Play the game.

GO ON IMMEDIATELY TO ACTIVITY 5

Activity 5: tackle individually

Write down brief answers to these questions:

(1) What do you think *the group* did?
(2) What did *you* actually do?
(3) How did *you* feel?
(4) What, if anything, stands out in your memory?
(5) What insights, if any, have you gained?

GO ON IMMEDIATELY TO ACTIVITY 6

Activity 6: tackle as a group

(1) Go round the group letting each person read out his or her notes from activity 5 in turn. *No one should comment upon what is said.*
(2) When everyone has had their turn, if it seems appropriate, continue the discussion.

Reflecting Upon the Nature of Conflict in Real Life

Clearly games such as 'Scoring Points' or 'Win as much as you can' may be seen as a model of the negotiation process. They do, however, have certain weaknesses since they assume that:

(1) All the players are equal in the sense that their positions are interchangeable. For example, whether you are in group A or group B does not, in principle, make any difference to the game itself.
(2) The players are 'collectively rational' in the sense that if they are and can co-ordinate their choices so that *both* parties can do better, they will.
(3) The range of actions available to each party can be specified precisely and be assigned tangible pay-off values.

It goes without saying, however, that hardly any of these assumptions, reasonable as they appear, can be satisfied in real-life conflict. In other words, it cannot be assumed that the parties involved are equal because how they define themselves is often a substantial issue of the conflict. It is difficult to hold a genuine debate with someone that you regard with contempt, for example. Neither can it be assumed that the actual 'issue' is the one expressed by the parties to the conflict for the actual issue may well be the structure of the system in which they are immersed; in which case the conflict is 'structure-orientated'. There are, then, limits to the types of conflict which can be modelled by such games. For conflicts which are about the actual issue expressed, i.e. 'issue-orientated' *and* which exist between parties who see themselves more or less as equals, the model does have something to offer. So can you now draw on that experience?

Activity 7: tackle individually

---

(1) Consider the nature of any conflict affecting your school-centred INSET. Would you classify it as 'issue-orientated' or 'structure-orientated'?
(2) Consider the other person or persons involved in the conflict. Do you consider all those involved to be equals?

Often conflicts which act as a hindrance to school-centred INSET are similar in structure to that modelled by 'Scoring Points' or 'Win as much as you can'. If, on reflection, this seems to be so for your particular situation, then the resolution of conflict will depend upon being able to find the points of common interest to those involved. On the other hand, if the conflict revolves around matters of structure, then the route to resolving the conflict will involve more 'political' strategies. Such techniques, which involve gaining influence and power, are discussed in 'The Myth of the Hero-innovator and Alternative Strategies for Organisational Change'.

Activity 8: tackle individually

The article 'The Myth of the Hero-innovator and Alternative Strategies for Organisational Change' is reproduced as Appendix II, pp. 161-8.

(1) Read the second section of the paper, pp. 164-7.
(2) Consider how appropriate these guidelines are for your situation.

Finding Ways of Resolving Conflict

When situations are interpreted as involving a conflict of interest, our behaviour tends to be based upon several assumptions viz:

(1) We must act in pursuit of our own self-interest.
(2) Everyone else will do likewise.
(3) We must act against the interest of others.
(4) Everyone else will be acting against our interests.

The result is that we trust no one, in turn this leads to poor communication and further misinterpretations. We are locked into the downward spiral of destructive conflict.

It is one thing to analyse a situation as one of 'destructive conflict', it is yet another actually to deal with it. Basically conflict can be ended in two ways:

(1) *by 'bargaining'*. Here, the requirement is for concessions from each party involved and it involves the idea of 'winning' or 'losing' or, more usually, 'compromise'. Strategies such as coercion and manipulation are at work; and as was pointed out earlier, these are rarely effective in relation to curriculum change; or

(2) *by mutual 'problem-solving'*. Here, the requirement is for each party to accept that there is no essential conflict of interest and it involves the idea that conflict is a subjectively defined, changeable phenomenon. As was suggested earlier, what matters here is that people work together to try and resolve a mutual problem.

The difficulty is that each of these approaches to ending conflict is characterised by very different behaviour. Whilst 'bargaining' requires adamant and directive behaviour with controlled communication; 'problem-solving' requires exploratory and tentative behaviour with open communication. These tend to be mutually inconsistent tactics, and adopting a problem-solving approach may hold out the possibility of generating new alternatives for action but it also increases vulnerability. So it is that, whilst both parties intellectually may see possibilities of co-operation, each rules them out because of the aggressive and non-cooperative behaviour of the other. Conflicts are rarely resolved without the help of a third party.

So far the activities in this chapter have helped you to consider various aspects of conflict and how, through the development of trust and openness, it is possible for symmetric, issue-orientated conflicts to move beyond the 'games' that are often a substitute for genuine communication. With some people – and in some situations – this may seem quite feasible. At this point, then, you may feel no further need to examine the roots of any conflict affecting your work; preferring, instead, to get on with the substantive task in hand. If, however, you feel that some further work would help resolve your particular conflict, then you may find it necessary to return to the theme of conflict resolution which is further discussed in Section 4, 'Change and Others', pp. 99-102.

Conflict may manifest itself in many ways and learning to handle it is difficult. Nevertheless, to ignore it is to invite the dangers of 'group-think'. The necessity to admit to conflict, however, is not only important in the context of relationships within the staff group. We all experience inner conflicts of some form or other, and we can only begin to try and resolve them if we are prepared to acknowledge that they even exist. This personal dimension is dealt with in Chapters 8 and 9.

SECTION TWO
CHANGING THE CURRICULUM

"Frankly, I don't see what the problem is . . . you seem quite normal to me . . ."

About This Section

In his autobiography (1973) Charlie Chaplin recalls a dinner at his home in California in 1926, at which Einstein, Mrs Einstein and two friends of Chaplin were present. At dinner Mrs Einstein related: 'The Doctor [i.e. Einstein] came down in his dressing gown as usual for breakfast, but he hardly touched a thing. I thought something was wrong, so I asked what was troubling him'. "Darling", he said, "I have a wonderful idea". And after drinking his coffee he went to the piano and started playing. Now and again he would stop, making a few notes and then repeat: "I've got a wonderful idea, a marvellous idea". I said: "Then for goodness sake tell me what it is, don't keep me in suspense". He said: "It's difficult, I still have to work it out".' Mrs Einstein told Chaplin that Einstein continued playing the piano and making notes for about half an hour, then went upstairs to his study, telling her that he did not wish to be disturbed, and remained there for two weeks. 'Each day I sent him up his meals', she said, 'and in the evening he would walk a little for exercise, then return to his work again. Eventually he came down from his study looking very pale. "That's it", he told me, wearily putting two sheets of paper on the table. And that was his theory of relativity.'

The process of having a wonderful idea and shaping it into form is integral to much of your school-centred INSET work. Sometimes everything seems to go well and that idea begins to come alive; at other times, despite all the good intentions, it seems that the idea is in danger of being extinguished. The purpose of this section is to help you and your colleagues by providing structured activities at critical points in the process of mutual problem-solving, which is the essence of changing the curriculum. In particular, we have suggested ways to approach:

- the selection of an issue to concentrate upon;
- the formulation of the problem itself;
- breaking down the problem into component parts and planning how to tackle them;
- collecting the necessary information for resolving the problem;
- establishing a resolution that really works for your school.

It involves the use of a methodical approach to problem-solving; helping you both to be more efficient in your actions and to evaluate more easily the effects of those actions. A considerable amount of literature on

25

problem-solving exists, and several different analyses of the stages of problem-solving have been attempted. The important thing is to find a method or 'heuristic' that works for you in your situation.

3 EXPLORING SCHOOL ISSUES

The Difficulty of Beginning

Perhaps for you it will be easy to start working with colleagues to problem-solve a relevant area of the life of your school. Most schools will have many such mutual issues, noticed and unnoticed, cared for and uncared for. The most difficult of those issues may have grown out of the easy ones that remained unnoticed and uncared for.

Possibly you will start with one issue and find yourselves drawn into others. The important thing, of course, is to get off to a good start. The purpose of this chapter is to help get things going. The suggestions represent merely some potential starting points for you and your colleagues to accept, adapt or reject. Basically, they involve either sharing concerns or experience – both are described here.

Unnoticed issues may later give rise to problems

Shared Concerns

For most of us, our anxieties and fears are important forces in shaping how we view the events of our daily experience. These are the 'hidden agendas' that we carry around with us. Often they remain hidden until revealed by a chance of circumstance, and yet they can be a useful starting point for change.

Activity 9: tackle individually

Describe two situations in your school which lead you to think that school-centred INSET might be helpful.
YOU WILL NEED TO TAKE THE RESULTS OF THIS ACTIVITY TO A GROUP MEETING.

Activity 10: tackle as a group

(1) Take it in turns to list and describe your results from activity 9 above.
(2) *On your own*, rank order all the items listed in terms of your own opinion of their importance for the school, e.g. number 1 for the most important item, number 2 for the second most important etc.
(3) Try, *as a group*, to come to a decision about the ranking of these items. It is important that each ranking be agreed upon by each group member before it becomes a part of the group decision; although not every ranking need meet with everyone's *complete* approval it should be one with which all group members can at least partially agree. During this process try to:

(a) avoid arguing for your own individual judgements;
(b) avoid changing your mind only in order to reach agreement and avoid conflict. Support only solutions with which you are able to agree to some extent;
(c) avoid, if possible, techniques such as majority vote or averaging;
(d) view differences of opinion as helpful rather than a hindrance in clarifying the group's thinking.

This activity should have helped the group to select an issue (or issues) to explore further. Do remember, however, not to be too ambitious in what you choose to tackle.

Shared Experience

An alternative starting point – or a more positive follow-up to sharing concerns – is to find something stimulating which will generate discussion around a particular curriculum issue. Everyone on the staff contains a rich store of ideas and experience – although usually this vast resource is not recognised. Often experience is so individual and idiosyncratic that some people find it difficult to make their experiences available to others. A shared experience can be interesting and provide a good framework for the exploration of past experience. Perhaps a piece of prose, a poem, a cartoon or a worksheet would be suitable. Whatever is chosen needs to be germane to the curriculum issue and likely to open up debate.

Activity 11: tackle individually

Appendices V-VIII, pp. 175-85 are an illustration of the sort of material that could provide the basis for such a shared experience as described above. They have been included because they cover a range of educational issues – project work, lesson content, English and mathematics – and a variety of materials. They are *not* intended to be appropriate in your context, but to give a flavour of what is involved.

(1) Examine the contents of Appendices V-VIII.
(2) Select a similar item which you think would be appropriate for your context.
(3) Jot down why you decided to choose it.

YOU WILL NEED TO TAKE THE RESULTS OF THIS ACTIVITY TO A GROUP MEETING

Activity 12: tackle as a group

Take it in turns to describe your results from activity 11 above.

This chapter should have helped you and your colleagues to start talking about issues concerning the life of your school. In Chapter 4 the activities will help you to examine the central problem more systematically.

4 CONSIDERING THE PROBLEM

The Importance of Problem Formulation

In the world of classrooms and schools each particular teaching and learning situation has its own practical problems and its own specific requirements. We know, for example, that our own effectiveness as teachers depends on what we are trying to teach and the types of pupils involved.

Each teaching and learning situation has its own problems and requirements

Similarly, if we are asked to change from teaching a subject with which we are familiar to one on which our knowledge is seriously limited, the move is far from effortless. There may be many reasons why this should be so, but the underlying point is the limitation for any teacher of a received solution to a problem formulated by someone else. In the final analysis it has to be each of us who, somehow or other, works out our own individual salvation for our own particular teaching situation. This does not mean that we do not need help, advice or guidance, but if we are to sort out a practical problem in our own classroom it has to be each of us who learns how to do so. Unless this happens, we are in the position of being offered (as Popper put it) 'unwanted answers to unasked questions'.

In this chapter you will find activities to support the process of problem-formulation. This is a vital but neglected and precarious part of problem-solving.

How a problem is defined will significantly affect the solutions eventually to be considered. No doubt you are familiar with the story of the lorry stuck under a bridge and blocking the road. The various suggestions offered by adults involved considerable damage either to the bridge or the lorry. It was a child who suggested letting some air out of the tyres. The child had not changed the facts but changed the way the facts were viewed. People who jump to conclusions are less likely to see any other definition of the problem. By spending time, at this stage, on defining (and possibly redefining) your problem and the critical elements that need changing to remedy it, you are more likely to achieve a workable solution.

Considering Constraints

In any institution, the way things are – or the *status quo* – will be the result of its historical development. Consequently, the context for your curriculum work will be made up of a complex interplay of forces. These forces may be people, resources, external factors, indeed, anything either hindering or helping change. You could picture the existing situation as in Figure 4.1 (p. 32). The net result of attempts to change the balance perhaps is little more than a heightened sense of frustration for all involved. Since the result of increasing the pressure to alter a situation is frequently an increased tension, any attempt to change the *status quo* needs to take account not only of the pressures for change but also those pressures constraining change. Only if the strengths of the latter are reduced is there much hope of success.

Even apparently specific problems are often only specific at first sight, and quickly become complex, many-faceted – even ill-defined – once you try to get a handle on them. Nevertheless, no matter how unsatisfactory a problem statement appears in hindsight, you need something to start the ball rolling.

Figure 4.1

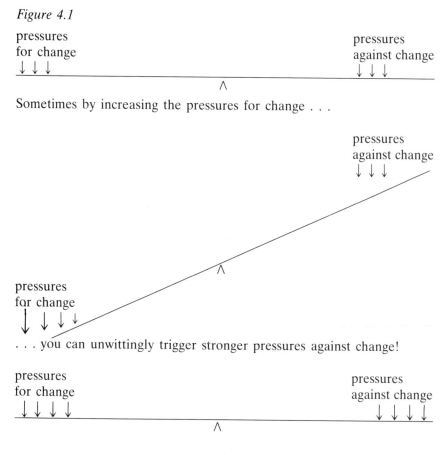

pressures
for change
↓ ↓ ↓

pressures
against change
↓ ↓ ↓

∧

Sometimes by increasing the pressures for change . . .

pressures
against change
↓ ↓ ↓

pressures
for change
↓ ↓ ↓ ↓

∧

. . . you can unwittingly trigger stronger pressures against change!

pressures
for change
↓ ↓ ↓ ↓

pressures
against change
↓ ↓ ↓ ↓

∧

Activity 13: tackle as a group

Think about the issue that you want to tackle in your school.

(1) Make a list of whatever seems to be working against change.
(2) Make a list of whatever seems to be working for change.
(3) From your list in (1) above, choose the two strongest items working against change. For each item, consider how you could possibly reduce or eliminate the pressure.
(4) Now, from your list in (2) above, choose the two strongest items working for change. For each item, consider how you could possibly build upon these.
(5) Try to formulate a suitable phrase to describe:

● the issue concerned
● what you want to do about it

For example, 'How to encourage sensible use of calculators by pupils'. Write down your problem statement.

(6) Re-examine your written statement, consider whether it limits the problem area unnecessarily to straightforward improvements without considering more fundamental solutions. If your problem statement seems too vague or too restrictive, alter it until it seems suitable.

Considering Appropriateness

It is important to find an issue with which you and your colleagues can grapple *at a level in which things can be changed*. In other words, don't begin with a problem which is much too large or ambitious. In order to help you clarify whether your problem (as described in activity 13) is appropriate, try testing it against this set of criteria:

● it has immediate, practical effects on the educational experience of the children;
● it is important to you and your colleagues and everyone wants or needs to tackle it;
● it can lead to some improvement of the situation by you and your colleagues;
● it has no known 'right' solution;
● it requires you and your colleagues to use your own ideas for solving the problem;
● it is one with which you and your colleagues feel able to cope and are reasonably confident of succeeding in the time available.

Activity 14: tackle as a group

---

(1) Review the set of criteria listed above and list any others which you need to consider.
(2) Test your problem (as described in activity 13) against the complete set of criteria. If necessary, re-frame your problem.

Brainstorming

A technique that you may find useful is called 'brainstorming'; it is simply a method for generating a wide range of ideas for tackling a stated problem. This is something we often want to do to make sure we are not overlooking particular parts of a problem, or particular solution areas, or sometimes just for getting started on a search for a way out of a difficult problem. You may want to use the 'brainstorming' technique with your colleagues. If you feel that the technique may be useful for you, here is how to proceed:

Procedure

(1) Allow 5-10 minutes for group members to write down their first ideas in response to the problem statement.

(2) Encourage group members to continue writing down new ideas, whilst each person in turn reads out one idea from his/her set. The session rules are:

   (a) No criticism is allowed of any idea
   (b) All ideas are quite welcome – even if they seem a bit far-fetched at first
   (c) A large number of ideas should be produced
   (d) Improvements on ideas already put forward should be included.

(3) Evaluate the ideas after the session. Often an idea, although not perfect, is also not totally useless. One way to develop such ideas is to:

   (a) describe the positive, favourable characteristics of the idea
   (b) describe any objections or concerns to the idea in a 'how to' form.

Comments

Use small record cards (or pieces of paper), with one idea expressed briefly on each card.

The session should be fun – a relaxed creative atmosphere.

Activity 15: tackle as a group

Using the idea of brainstorming, your group should:

(1) Review both your problem statement and lists of things working for and against change from activity 13.

(2) On small cards or pieces of paper, write down all the thoughts that occur to you, as they occur to you, in response to your problem statement. You will need these cards for the next activity.

Classifying

Another helpful technique at this stage is classification since this may reveal the underlying structure of a problem, or at least suggest directions for what to do next. If you want to try this technique, here is how to proceed:

Procedure	*Comments*
(1) Record each collected item of information on a separate card (or piece of paper).	This can be done whilst collecting information, e.g. by writing ideas on cards during Brainstorming.
(2) Familiarise yourself with the collected set of cards, by reading through them a few times.	You will need a large, undisturbed working surface.
(3) Sort and resort the cards into categories until a classification is found which satisfies the following rules:	Stop as soon as you have a system that will serve your immediate purpose, even if it is not perfect.

    (a) It fits your current view of the problem
    (b) All the cards are included in the classification
    (c) There are only very few, if any, cards which could be placed in more than one of the categories
    (d) The number of categories is a manageable size
    (e) The classification provides a useful guide to further action.

The reason for attempting a classification is that it imposes a convenient pattern on what might otherwise be a random collection of data, so that major areas are defined for further action. It is important to remember that classification is a stepping-stone to action rather than a search for logical elegance.

Activity 16: tackle as a group

(1) Using your cards from activity 15, your group should try this classification procedure until

● you have the cards set out in a classification you are happy with, and
● in which almost every card fits obviously, to you, into its category and could not equally well be in any other of the categories

(2) Record your classification on a large sheet of paper like this:

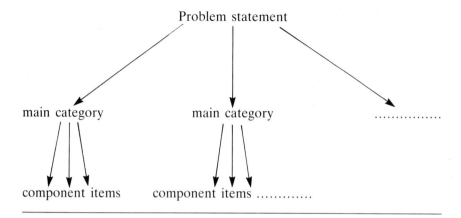

Making the Problem Manageable

By now you should have some idea of your objective, any likely obstacles to be confronted, and some of the possible tasks ahead of you. If you feel that you have formulated the problem satisfactorily, then you should begin planning, in broad terms, how to tackle it. There are likely to be stages where an individual or a small group could usefully work on their own, and stages where it is important that the whole group should participate and make decisions.

Activity 17: tackle as a group

(1) Determine the most promising steps you could take towards resolving the problem and the resources available to you.
(2) In the light of (1) above, break down what needs to be done into manageable components, and share out responsibility for undertaking the work throughout the group so that the best use is made of each person's time and talents.

Before Moving on

It is worth considering, before proceeding any further, the ways in which people can keep regularly in touch so that no sub-group goes off at a total tangent without everyone knowing. Isolation and totally independent action usually gives rise to unnecessary conflict.

This chapter should have helped you to review the problem-area very thoroughly so that your problem-definition is based upon as considered a view as possible. When we begin thinking about problems we always start from our own prejudices. This is inevitable; the danger only begins if we fail to move beyond them. That is why we have stressed the need to:

(1) Consider constraints – because your problem does not exist in a vacuum.
(2) Formulate the problem appropriately – so that it is at a level in which action can be taken.
(3) Generate a wide range of ideas for tackling the problem – to avoid 'tunnel vision'.
(4) Break the problem down into manageable parts – so that you can see a way forward for actually tackling it.

Usually this stage takes much longer than people anticipate, but it is time and effort well invested. Even so, later on you may find it becomes necessary to redefine the problem as a result of further insights. Don't be dismayed if this should happen, it can be a valuable aspect of problem-solving. In Chapter 5 the activities are intended to help you plan your approach to tackling the problem in more detail.

5 TACKLING THE COMPONENTS OF THE PROBLEM

Thinking of Ideas for Resolving the Problem

So far you have made a start by attempting to formulate the problem into a form with which you can cope.

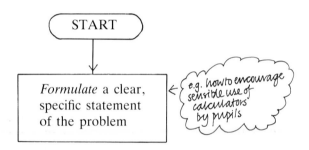

By now you are probably beginning to have ideas about what might be done. It is these ideas that you need to examine to see if they will really resolve your particular problem. The more specific your ideas the better they can be tested. In flow-chart form, what you need to do now is shown in Figure 5.1 (p. 39).

Building on the Brainstorming

The work that you did for activity 15 will provide a good basis for thinking through what needs to be done. So far the cards will have been classified into groups, each of which represents a separate component of the problem. Each of those groups of cards now needs to go through a process of refinement if it is to be really useful. A real problem is rather like an onion, you need to keep peeling away the layers to get to the core, and doing so may bring tears to your eyes! In effect, you need to

Figure 5.1

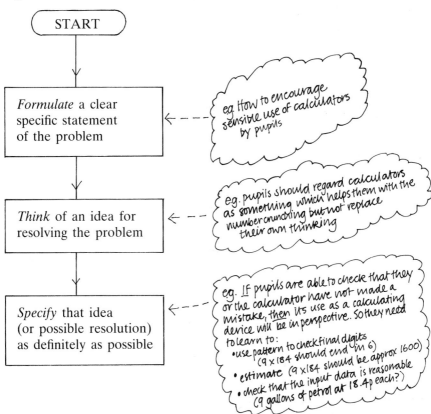

You may need to go through this procedure of idea-specification for each separate component of your problem – either as a sub-group, or an individual or, possibly, as a whole group.

move from superficial aspects through possible perspectives to the heart of your problem. Here is how to proceed:

Procedure

(1) Identify the key factors by reviewing the original cards using these criteria:

    (a) Is it expressed as a single idea?
    (b) Is it expressed so that it relates directly to our purpose?
    (c) Is it brief and precise?
    (d) Is it stated in neutral terms?

(2) Alter or discard any items that do not meet the above criteria, e.g. 'Pupils must

Comments

Use your original brainstorming cards or generate some more concerning your particular component of the problem.

You should be moving from random thoughts about the matter to well-formed use existing knowledge as well as a calcu-lator' might become 'Use tables to check digits' *and* 'use skill of estimation'.

(3) Scan the cards that you now have to see if some seem to be linked to others. Cluster together those cards for which you perceive a relationship. Keep in mind that:

> (a) small clusters might be more useful than large ones because their focus may be sharper;
> (b) a card may be included in more than one cluster;
> (c) a cluster might suggest that a new card needs to be made and incorporated.

(4) Examine each cluster produced, study it carefully and ask yourself 'What is it trying to tell me?'

statements accurately expressing what you consider to be relevant to the initial problem.

Don't worry if you cannot express a cluster relationship in words or give a rational justification for it. At this stage you may intuitively sense a link worth exploring.

This stage may give a number of different perspectives on the problem and a better idea of what to do to resolve it.

Activity 18: tackle on your own or as a sub-group

Using the procedure described above:

(1) Review the random thoughts on your component of the problem from the brainstorming session.
(2) Produce clusters of what you consider are the significant factors.
(3) Examine your clusters and describe your idea for resolving the aspect of the problem as definitely as possible.
(4) Write down your description and check that it does contain specific information.

Raising Questions

Your ideas need to be systematically examined in order to see how realistic they are for the problem – in other words, will they really work? The way to do this is to consider what questions need to be asked about your ideas. If, after investigation, they fail the test on any of these questions then maybe they weren't such good ideas after all!

Finding the right questions to ask helps to give a strong purpose to your investigation and assists with collecting the essential information. Often it is easiest to tackle this as a two-stage process:

● a creative phase during which you generate questions which you hope to look at more closely;
● a critical phase during which you select those questions most likely to yield something definite.

You may need to go through this process more than once until you have suitable questions, e.g.

● Are there any activities which encourage pupils to 'make single digit pattern checks'?
● Will calculator games such as 'Bullseye' encourage pupils to estimate before calculating?
● Can we find enough suitable problems using realistic data to encourage 'input data checks'?

Activity 19: tackle on your own or as a sub-group

In relation to the idea described in activity 18

(1) Write down some possible questions for investigation.
(2) Re-examine your questions and consider:

● whether they will actually help you achieve your purpose; and
● whether they really can be investigated.

If necessary, alter them until they are suitable.

Preparing to Collect Information

The first point, of course, is to ensure that the information you collect will actually answer the questions. This means checking that you have:

● taken account of all the variables (or things) involved;
● defined them in terms which makes them observable or measurable (you must have some way to know when you have answered your question!);
● considered the size of sample to be involved, e.g. is observation of *one* lesson enough?.

Once you have done this and designed your investigation, you will need to consider how you will collect the information. For example, you may decide to use classroom observations, visits to see existing practice in other schools, external expertise or perhaps to look through the available literature.

Activity 20: tackle on your own or as a sub-group

---

(1) Review the questions you formulated in activity 19.
(2) Note how you think that you will collect the information for each question.

Checking with Colleagues

By now you will have quite definite plans about how to tackle your part of the problem. Before carrying out your plans, however, you need to check with your colleagues to get some feedback on what you intend to do.

Activity 21: tackle as a group

---

(1) Share the results of your planning from activities 18-20 with your colleagues.
(2) If necessary, revise your plans in the light of their comments.

This chapter should have helped you to generate, select and develop ideas in relation to your problem. The value of such planning is that the better you can specify your idea, the easier it becomes to identify systematically the faults, weaknesses and difficulties within it. The limitation is that planning can help us to deal only with conditions and variables which we already know or suspect are important. It is still possible for plans to be invalidated to a greater or lesser extent when hitherto unimportant or unknown variables are seen to impinge upon the problem. In Chapter 6 the activities are intended to help you with the collection and analysis of relevant information.

6 COLLECTING INFORMATION

Sources of Information and Their Use

This chapter deals with three important sources of information for curriculum development work:

- classroom observation;
- visits to other classrooms or schools;
- external expertise.

Depending upon both your problem and your circumstances, you may need to draw on one or more of these sources for useful information.

It is important that this investigative stage is undertaken so that there is no uncritical acceptance of a proposed resolution, which, when implemented, proves to be quite inappropriate for your school. In flow-chart form, what you will be doing is shown in Figure 6.1 (p. 44). The activities are designed to help you and your colleagues with this part of the problem-solving process. Having achieved a clear formulation of the problem in the previous chapters, you may have either:

- a wide range of possible resolutions that you want to consider, or
- a possible resolution with several different aspects needing to be investigated.

This may mean that your group divides into sub-groups in order to tackle the various tasks (such as one of the possible resolutions or a particular aspect of a resolution). Clearly, this chapter is applicable to each of the various tasks, and should be used as a guide to the work by any sub-groups or individuals.

The Need for Flexibility

Before you embark upon activities, do remember that the process of solving a real problem, from the initial discontent with an existing state of affairs through to a satisfactory resolution, is rarely smooth. Initial strategies for dealing with a complex problem are often inadequate and may lead to frustrating dead ends. The value of these cul-de-sacs is that

Figure 6.1

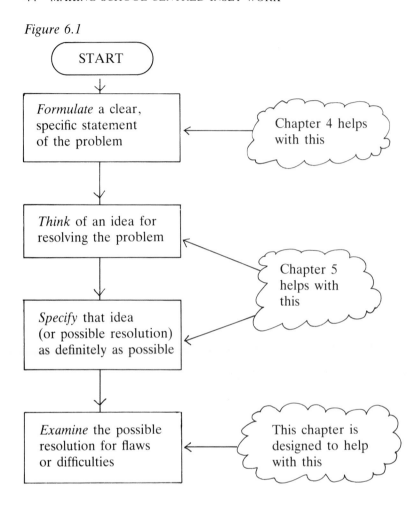

they usually provide new insights into the nature of the problem. Getting stuck and going back to an earlier stage in the process – or 'looping – is inherent in problem-solving, and only the inexperienced problem-solver sees it as 'failure'. When working with such a dynamic process, whose very essence is flexibility, it is important to be wary of any formalisations of the problem-solving process into a predetermined series of steps. In this text there *is* linear progression through the activities, but that should not be taken to imply that, in practice, the process will be like this:

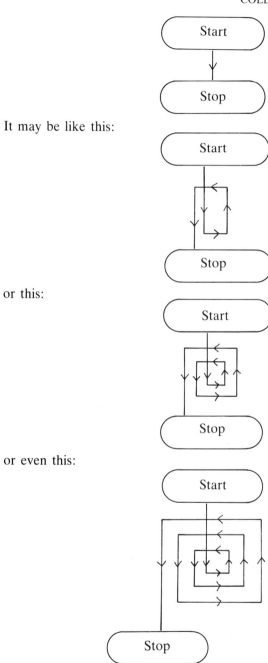

It may be like this:

or this:

or even this:

Provided that you have confidence in your own ability to resolve the problem, you will eventually arrive at a satisfactory resolution!

Classroom Observation

Throughout our day-to-day interaction with those that we teach, what *we* do is influenced, either consciously or not, by a process of gathering and processing information. We look at the way someone tackles something, listen to what they say and discuss things with them. This way of getting feedback can be called 'observation' and helps us, as teachers, to become more sensitive to the actual learning being experienced by our pupils. Most of the time we do this as a matter of course, not even making any formal record of what we observe.

Observation includes discussing and listening as well as looking

As teachers, we often underrate the importance of our own classrooms. If reading books has its place in helping us to reflect upon our practice as teachers, then so too does 'reading' the phenomena taking place in our own classrooms. On occasion, a conscious attempt to collect and record classroom observations can provide us with windows into the realities of our classroom practice. Such windows also give us the opportunity for looking at familiar phenomena in new ways, especially if we feel capable of sharing the data with colleagues and listening to their suggestions of how it may be interpreted.

Observing the 'curriculum in action' – or the curriculum as it really exists in the classroom through the actual experience of the pupils – takes practice. A detailed elaboration of this approach to curriculum evaluation can be found in the Open University's *Curriculum in Action* materials (Merritt *et al.*, 1980). The following procedure, however, should help you to get started.

Procedure

(1) *Decide WHAT* to observe. This is likely to be determined by the plans that you made in Chapter 5. For example, the question 'Will calculator games such as "Bullseye" encourage pupils to estimate before calculating?'

(2) *Decide WHO* to observe. Do not be over ambitious or your observations may be very superficial. It is often more productive to focus on a small group of pupils to observe in detail rather than a whole class. You will probably find it quite difficult at first to keep your attention on the pupils you want to observe. To a certain extent this is inevitable, but with practice and conscious effort, you will be able to be more systematic.

(3) *Decide WHEN* to observe. Carry out your teaching as usual, but plan for short periods of time when you are observing your pupils, rather than working with them. Sometimes, it will be easy for you to stand back and observe what they are doing. On other occasions, it will be more difficult. Try to plan and organise your classroom work so that it may be possible to withdraw from actual teaching for a short time in order to observe the pupils. After all, it is not unusual for a teacher to have to turn his or her attention from interacting with the pupils for a while.

(4) *Decide HOW* to observe. Your methods of recording your observations will vary. However, do try to make quick jottings of everything you see happening. (You may find later that it has a significance that you did not realise at first.) You will probably discover that you need to devise some kind of personal shorthand in order to make notes in the classroom. Experiment with your system until you are satisfied that it is comprehensive enough to enable you to record everything which is likely to happen. As soon as possible after the lesson try to write down those things which you remember happening, but which for some reason you could not record at the time. Add these to your classroom notes. Be as specific and factual as possible when making your on-the-spot notes and the additional notes made after the lesson. This will be helpful when you later analyse your observations.

However discreetly you think you are making notes, some pupils are almost bound to notice that you are doing something unusual. You will need to decide whether to explain to them what you are doing or not.

Your ability to make observations in the classroom improves with practice. You may feel that, with hindsight, there are some things that you did when observing that you should not have done, and some things that you didn't do which you wish you had done. For this reason, it is best to have a 'trial run' at classroom observation which you can then reflect upon so that you can hone up your observation techniques.

Activity 22: tackle individually

---

(1) Considering the question 'What did the pupils actually do?', decide on the most appropriate way of making observations for yourself in your own classroom.
(2) Carry out the observation in your own classroom.
(3) After you have finished your observations, ask your pupils to look back over the same period and answer the question 'What did I actually do?'

Activity 23: tackle the first part on your own, but the second part with at least one colleague

---

(1) Consider the procedure that you used for making your classroom observations in activity 22.

   (a) what improvements would you make now for carrying out a second set of observations?
   (b) what difficulties did you experience for which you still cannot see any solution?

(2) Discuss, with a colleague, your observation procedure and your responses to both questions above.
(3) Plan how you will carry out another observation in your classroom.

Activity 24: tackle individually

---

(1) Review your work for activities 20 and 21.
(2) Use the procedure described above to plan and carry out the necessary classroom observations for collecting information about your problem.

Analysing Classroom Observations

The information gleaned from your classroom may contain a number of useful messages. The art of analysing classroom observations is to gain access to as many of those messages as possible. One way of doing this is physically to manipulate your raw data so that your analysis becomes dynamic, able to provide a constantly shifting picture of interpretations. Here is how to proceed:

Procedure

(1) Categorise your observations. Try starting with the headings 'Things the pupils did which I intended' and 'Things the pupils did which I did not intend'. Then try sorting the observations under some different headings. As you sort other headings or sub-headings will occur to you. Keep a note of your groupings as you go.

(2) Check any inferences made. Look again at your categorisations. Could you answer the question 'How did you know?'? If you were asked to explain why you chose to put your observations under certain headings could you? Look for alternative interpretations or inferences that could be made on the basis of the evidence available.

(3) Review what your pupils said. As well as carrying out your observations, you may well have asked your pupils to consider the question 'What did I actually do?' Now that you think you have a picture of what was going on during that period, have another look at what they said they experienced. Are there any comments there that surprise you?

Comments

Write out each observation on a separate slip of paper or small cards so that the information is represented concretely and is always available for visual scanning. This stage will help to clarify your information, highlight issues and reveal patterns.

Inferences can be made at all stages:

● observation;
● recording of observations;
● categorisation of observations.

It is important to try to detect when inferences have been made so that they may be checked.

Activity 25: tackle individually

(1) Use the procedure described above to analyse your classroom observations from activity 24.
(2) Write a brief account of this work describing:

● what insights, if any, you gained;
● its contribution towards resolving the problem.

YOU WILL NEED TO TAKE THE RESULTS OF THIS ACTIVITY TO A GROUP MEETING

Activity 26: tackle as a group

Share your account of your work from activity 25 with your colleagues.

Joint Classroom Observations

Many of us feel anxious at the thought of having another teacher observe us at work, yet it can provide the basis for a very helpful discussion. In view of this, the following two activities should only be undertaken by mutual agreement of those involved. It is important that both teachers should feel 'comfortable' about the activity. For example, before you begin, agree where your observer will be positioned in the classroom and what he or she will do.

Activity 27: tackle with a colleague

---

(1) Agree with a colleague how you will jointly try to find answers to the question under investigation. For example, you may find it helpful to observe for 10 minutes each during a lesson.
(2) Carry out your observations in the classroom.

During the observations themselves you will each have collected on-the-spot notes. As soon as possible afterwards, work together to analyse the observations in the way suggested on pp. 48-9.

Activity 28: tackle with a colleague

---

(1) Analyse your notes by

- categorising the observations;
- checking any inferences made;
- looking for alternative ways of interpreting the observations.

(2) Write a brief account of your observations describing:

- what insights, if any, you gained from the work;
- its contribution towards resolving the problem.

YOU WILL NEED TO TAKE THE RESULTS OF THIS ACTIVITY TO A GROUP MEETING

Activity 29: tackle as a group

Share your account from activity 28 with your colleagues.

Visits to Other Classrooms and to Other Schools

The practice of 'visiting' other teachers' classrooms, either in your own school or another school, is a well-established form of in-service activity experienced by many teachers at some point in their careers.

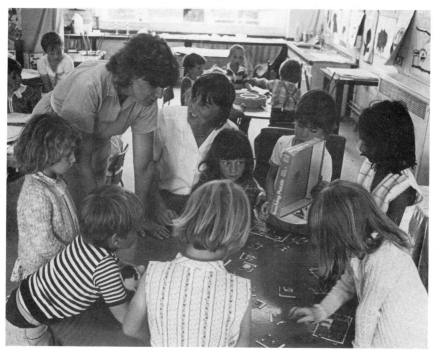

Visits to other classrooms can be refreshing

Such visits can be very refreshing, enabling both observations of practice in another school and discussion with host teachers in order to place that practice in a meaningful context.

Shostak (1982) provides a timely reminder, however, of a possible difficulty of arranging such visits to observe 'good practice':

> teachers may sense that the gap between the observed practice and their own is pretty substantial and they may not automatically see how to translate what they have seen into a specification for their own action. If one is struggling, and conscious of struggling, it may not be helpful to see other teachers, in apparently similar situations, accomplishing a similar task with elegant ease.

In the same study she also suggests the following checklist for arranging a visit to another school:

1. Identify an area of concern in your own practice or in the school's practice.
2. Clarify the purpose of the visit.
3. Consider whether more than one visit is both viable and feasible.
4. Consider the time of year of the visit (i.e. is the end of term a sensible time?).
5. Collect information which will help you decide which school to approach. (Information might come from advisers, teachers' centre leaders, colleagues – anyone with personal knowledge of the schools.)
6. Make arrangements for the cover of your classes.
7. Make arrangements with the host school (it seems better if the visiting teacher can do this him – or herself) and offer adequate information about your concerns:

> explain the purpose of the visit
> identify a convenient day and time of day to arrive
> find out about the timetable on the day of visiting
> be clear at what time school starts and finishes
> try to make some contact with all those who will be involved (i.e. the class teacher and the headteacher)
> see if you can find out whether there will be time for discussion with teachers you wish to talk to.

8. Brief yourself about the school as fully as you can.
9. Make a list of questions relevant to your area of concern. Think how to gather data/information that will illuminate your question, and think how to record this while you are in the school.
10. Establish what you are going to do during the following events: assembly; hall time; morning and afternoon breaks; dinner-time; immediately after school.
11. After the visit, take time to reflect on your experience and to think about its application. You may want to organise your impressions in notes.
12. Feedback to your professional colleagues is important: has your head made some arrangement for talking to you about your visit, or for you to make a report, fairly formally, to staff? (Have your thoughts well organised if you are to make a formal presentation; sometimes a written and duplicated agenda not only helps to focus discussion but gives colleagues an opportunity to consider the issues themselves before the meeting.)
13 Encourage staff interest in any subsequent follow-up and implementation.
14. Offer some account to the host school of the way the visit has been used so that they feel that the effort they made was worthwhile.

Activity 30: tackle on your own or as a sub-group

---

(1) Review the checklist suggested by Shostak above, and consider items 1-5 in relation to your own work for activities 20 and 21.
(2) Decide whether a visit to another classroom or another school still seems both an appropriate *and* a possible way of collecting the information that you need. If it does seem to be, then, bearing in mind the other items in Shostak's checklist, plan your approach in detail and carry out the visit.

Activity 31: tackle on your own or as a sub-group

Write a brief account of your visit to another classroom or another school describing:

(a) What you learned from the visit.
(b) Its contribution towards resolving the problem.

YOU WILL NEED TO TAKE THE RESULTS OF THIS ACTIVITY TO A GROUP MEETING

Activity 32: tackle as a group

Share your account of your work from activity 31 with your colleagues.

External Expertise

Historically, members of LEA advisory services have always provided some form of INSET within schools, e.g. working alongside teachers, attending staff meetings or running workshops. In recent years this resource has been supplemented by members of staff of higher and further education institutions and by other local teachers. Provided that the 'outsider' involved has high credibility in the eyes of the participants, such a person can be a useful resource for school-centred INSET activity. The outsider can, for example, provide reassurance and confidence for a staff, or give inspiration through a new perspective on something of interest.

Activity 33: tackle either as a sub-group or with the whole group

---

(1) Consider the educational issue which is the basis for your school-

centred INSET activity, e.g. 'record-keeping for reading'. Briefly discuss:

(a) The advantages and disadvantages of group members telling each other their experiences in this field.
(b) What would have been gained and lost if an expert in the field had been brought in to talk to you in the first session on this subject.

(2) Consider when, if at all, you would want to bring in an expert in the field, and why.
(3) Review your work for activities 20 and 21. Consider whether 'external expertise' would be an appropriate way of furthering your thinking at this stage. If so, write down:

● *Who* you would like to use from outside;
● *How* you would envisage making use of their experience and expertise.

(4) Plan your use of external expertise in detail and then carry it out.

Activity 34: tackle on your own or as a sub-group

Write a brief account of your use of external expertise describing:

(a) What you learned from the 'outsider'.
(b) Its contribution towards resolving the problem.

YOU WILL NEED TO TAKE THE RESULTS OF THIS ACTIVITY TO A GROUP MEETING

Activity 35: tackle as a group

Share your account of your work from activity 34 with your colleagues.

Being Prepared to Re-frame the Problem

This chapter should have helped you to collect and analyse the necessary information for resolving your particular problem. If, during the process, your perception of that problem has changed, then you may need to return to the activities in the earlier chapters in order to redefine either the problem itself or your approach to it. In Chapter 7 the activities are intended to help you decide upon a workable resolution and put it into action.

7 ESTABLISHING A SUCCESSFUL RESOLUTION

Murphy's Warning

Analysis of information is one thing, interpreting the implications into a workable resolution for your particular problem is quite another! Everyone needs both the time to review what the working groups have produced and the opportunity to air their own thoughts and feelings, before considering exactly what is to be done.

Negative as it may sound, a helpful way to approach this stage of the process is to ask 'What could go wrong?' By asking and answering this question, you can attempt to avoid errors resulting from an incomplete analysis of the resolution. Such an approach is, perhaps, best encapsulated in 'Murphy's Laws'. These are set out below as a reminder.

'Murphy's Laws'

A set of maxims that seems to fill the gaps between all the laws, rules, and regulations governing and explaining human behaviour:

> If anything can go wrong, it will.
> Nothing is as simple as it seems.
> Everything takes longer than you expect.
> If you fool around with something long enough, it will eventually break.
> If you try to please everybody, somebody is not going to like it.
> It is a fundamental law of nature that nothing ever quite works out.
> Whatever you want to do, you have to do something else first.
> It's easier to get into a thing than to get out of it.
> If you explain something so clearly that no one can misunderstand, someone will.

At its most pessimistic you might find as a group that all of the work produced to date doesn't really resolve the problem, and that you might have to get more information, re-think the approach or even start again from scratch. On the other hand . . .

Deciding on Appropriateness

There are limits to the rationality of any decision-making process. Nevertheless, some attempt to approach this in a structured way does ensure that we consciously clarify the values that we use as filters for the information at our disposal. If we do that then not only will we know *what* course of action we have decided upon but also *why*. If you want to tackle decision-making in a structured manner, here is one way to proceed:

Procedure

(1) List the options available to you. Perhaps, for example, there are several possible methods of record keeping to consider.

(2) Identify what you are concerned about when deciding between the options. For example, 'Easy to record information', 'Can be used for diagnostic teaching' and so on. These will be the attributes or criteria important for your decision.

(3) Draw up a simple matrix and list on it the options available and the attributes needed. For example,

Comments

Possible options are likely to have been identified during the stage of collecting information.

This stage really involves clarifying exactly why you prefer one option to another. It means talking it through, since often you might like different aspects of different options, but have not articulated exactly what it is that you like.

This helps to hold the set of criteria explicitly in focus.

Attributes needed

(4) Decide on the relative importance of the attributes by asking yourself 'Are there some attributes that matter more than others?' For example, you might feel that 'Can be used for diagnostic teaching' is twice as important as 'Easy to record information'.

(5) Examine each option against each attribute using a rating system. At this stage you will need to draw on the detailed information collected during Chapter 6. For example,

You can weight the attributes by any factor you like. For example, ×2, ×3 or even ×10. What matters is that your weighting is consistent with what you value.

This enables the information collected to be evaluated systematically in the light of the perceived requirements of your school.

	Attributes needed		
	Easy to record information	Can be used for diagnostic teaching ×2 →)	
Options available — Record system A	3	5(×2) (10)	
Record system B	5	4(×2) (8)	
↓			

(rated on a scale 1-5)

Activity 36: tackle as a group

Use the procedure described above to come to a decision about the most appropriate resolution for your problem.

At this point, any proposed resolutions may have been found to be inappropriate for your situation. If this is the case, you will need either to

● modify a possible resolution so that it does seem suitable, or
● reformulate your problem in the light of what you now know.

Either way you will experience that phenomenon described in the introduction to Chapter 6 as 'looping'. On the flow chart it will look as in Figure 7.1 (p. 58). On the other hand, a resolution may seem suitable, in which case you will need to implement it.

Into Action

By now you should be in a position to know:

● what needs to be communicated to other people about the proposed course of action (e.g. parents);
● what actually needs to be done to get the resolution working.

However, at the same time as considering the details of implementation, do think about how the resolution might need to be monitored in order to ensure that the problem is resolved, or at least ameliorated.

The sort of questions needing consideration at this stage are

● Who has overall responsibility for implementation?
● Is there any mechanism for reviewing progress? If not, how is this best done and by whom?
● What resources are needed to sustain the work started?

Figure 7.1

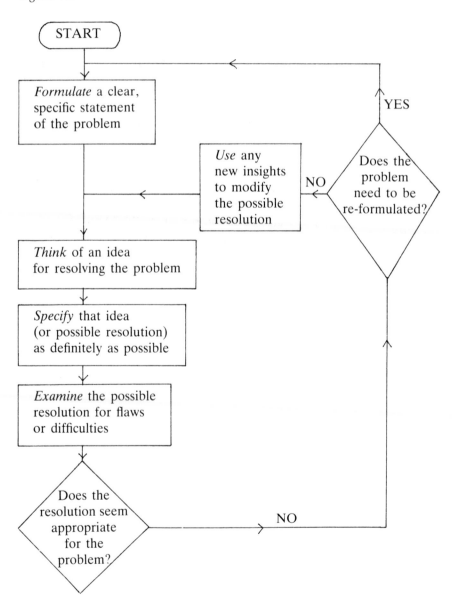

Activity 37: tackle as a group

---

(1) Consider what still needs to be done to ensure a smooth implementation of your resolution.
(2) Plan how the resolution will be monitored in action.

Final Thoughts

This chapter should have helped you to think through the details of implementing any proposed resolution so that it actually works in your context. Reference was made earlier to 'Murphy's Laws'; anyone who thinks that there is no truth in them might have found the activities in this chapter unnecessarily obvious. In which case, don't say later that you were not warned!

This section, 'Changing the Curriculum', has focused on some of the main component tasks you may encounter as you and your colleagues work on a mutual curriculum problem. In flow-chart form, the whole process looks as in Figure 7.2 (p. 60).

By now, the temptation may be to put the whole thing behind you as a job well done. Of course, that may be so, but do try to find time to reflect upon your experience throughout this work – that really will be the key to 'Making school-centred INSET work'. Section 5, 'Overview', should help you with this.

Figure 7.2

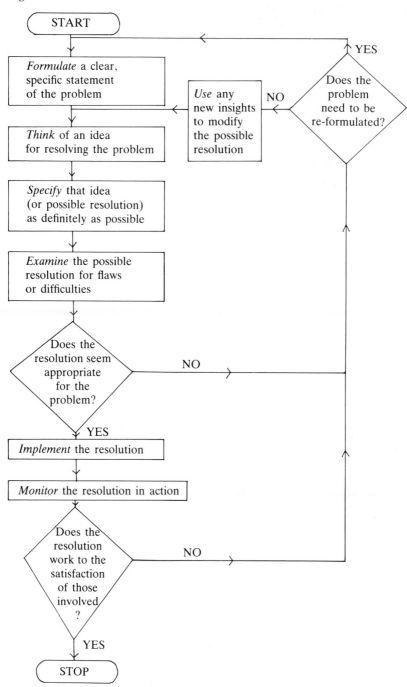

SECTION THREE
CHANGE AND YOU

When I take 5C
I'm masterful...

When I address
the P.T.A.,

I'm all eloquence
and
persuasion...

When I harangue
the whole school
I'm imperious...

I feel
THREATENED.

But when
Edith Balmer
won't wear
her
school tie...

About This Section

Often when we are forced by circumstances or events to make a critical appraisal of what we do and, by implication, the assumptions underlying our roles, priorities and beliefs, our strongest emotions come into play. The 'knock-on' effect of a curriculum change may touch things which are often closely linked with our very concept of ourselves. So we may react with denial, anger or despair – probably with each in turn – before either confronting or accepting something with the consequent change in self-concept and perspective which is appropriate to the new circumstances. Different people react in different ways: we may act as if nothing crucial is happening; we may strive to fight the forces of change or we may just become apathetic. No wonder then that curriculum development is so difficult.

This section considers what happens when, both as professionals and as adults, we experience or learn something which challenges the reality we have created through our thoughts. Its purpose is to help you examine the personal implications of curriculum change; some of the ways in which people may react to the stress that it generates, and possible ways of coping with this in a positive manner.

The activities are organised into three chapters:

● professional learning (you will find it useful to work through this chapter with a few other people);
● personal learning;
● transforming professional realities.

Classrooms are busy places; they are full of problems, successes and failures requiring immediate and effective action on our part as teachers. Our most obvious concern as teachers is the effect of our actions on our pupils. Each working day we see our pupils, each day we intuitively monitor what happens, each day we are reminded of the effects. We are not merely the users of someone else's curriculum ideas and materials in our own classrooms; we create the individuality that marks one classroom out as different from another and, through our constant decision-making, we actively shape the curriculum that our pupils actually experience. Any change in that curriculum experience is linked in some way to a change on our own part as teachers – in the way we act, the way we think, the materials we decide to introduce and so on. We may be confronted by

Teachers actively shape the curriculum that the pupils actually experience

something preventing us from achieving something we want to do. This conflict of circumstances and motives generates problems for us – and usually these are only solved by learning something new. Curriculum development in our classrooms, then, is usually a function of professional development on our own part as the teacher – and often that in turn is a function of our development as a person.

Identifying the link between educational change, professional development and personal development is difficult. The example of Nancy, a very experienced primary teacher, is a good illustration of this. Here she describes things that she did differently in her classroom as a consequence of in-service work:

> The first thing that strikes me now is how much I imposed upon children. I planned and prepared schemes, lessons and materials, told the children what to do, noted whether they had done it or not and grumbled or praised as necessary. Now I realise how important is the ability to choose – children should be given a chance to develop this

ability. For example, this term I took my class out to do a traffic/pedestrian survey. We were following a television programme which aims to develop their understanding of 'a street'. Previously *I* would have chosen the locality, the groups, the time and I would have prepared a sheet on which they would record their findings. I didn't do any of those things, we made the decisions together using maps from the Local Studies Library, our own school timetable and our own list of what we would be counting.

This changed attitude on Nancy's part towards *what* her pupils are permitted to do and *how* was also noted by Jill, a colleague of Nancy. She confirmed that this aspect of Nancy's classroom life was different:

> she relies less and less on distributing material for them to learn from. I would say she tries to put them into situations where they have got to assess what they know, what they want to find out and formulate their own way of finding that out.

Clearly Nancy has made a deep-rooted change in her classroom practice and, in doing so, has effected some sort of change in herself and how she sees things. Her colleague, Jill, considered that Nancy had become more

Finding out for themselves

critically aware both of herself:

> she's changed her attitude towards herself, about her own future, I hadn't thought about that. Before, she was content and she has suddenly become more ambitious for herself

and of how she performed as a teacher:

> she is more adventurous, she is now prepared to try things and see if they fail and not just stick to things she feels will be safe . . . When things go wrong and they don't turn out or when she has doubts about what she's doing she seems to have more to fall back on. She seems to have set up strategies whereby she can think through what she is doing and come to some sort of conclusion to go one way or the other. Whereas before I felt that she resorted to despair now I feel that Nancy has developed strategies to get herself out of that situation.

Change, then, can be unpredictable. Start off by changing one thing and, without realising it, you may change a host of things which you had not even thought of – including yourself. In fact, the only certainty seems to be that no one can guarantee that they can bring about real change in another person's teaching no matter what their power or authority.

8 PROFESSIONAL LEARNING

What Does Learning Involve?

Many of us spend the vast proportion of our professional lives working with children and helping them to learn. It is easy to forget that, as professionals, there are times when we are also learners. It is even easier to forget what may be involved in such learning. We all have a fundamental need for self-esteem, so we don't want to be seen to fail. On the other hand, real learning involves taking risks. The confident learner is not the person who knows he or she will not fail, it is the person who knows that they can survive their failures, and therefore be prepared to risk them.

Learning is a life-long process. When we learn as adults it is invariably as a response to the motives and needs created by the tasks of adulthood as we see them at any particular time. Although the prevailing view of 'learning' in our society is that learning involves the explicit acquisition of a body of 'right' knowledge; many people sense intuitively that this view of learning is limited. This comes through in statements such as learning 'in the University of Life' and is an implicit recognition of a different type of learning which has a much more personal impact upon us.

In fact, there are many different types of learning, each of which most of us experience at some time in our lives. One may be about learning how to do something, another may be about learning how something relates to something else, another may be about learning how to cope with other people, and yet another may be about learning more about yourself and the influences that govern your life.

Activity 38: tackle individually

Review your own experience of learning as an adult. Find two examples of your own for each of the following types of learning:

(1) learning how to do something;
(2) learning how something relates to something else;
(3) learning how to cope with other people;
(4) learning more about yourself and the influences that govern your life.

Activity 39: tackle as a group

---

(1) Share your results from activity 38.
(2) Compare the different types of learning and the items within them.

For each category, consider whether there is anything distinctive involved in the type of learning described by that category. If so, make a note of it.

One point worth remembering is that different kinds of learning relate to different aspects of your life and may involve different ways of learning. For example, when we enter teaching as a probationer we have to learn how to do countless things related to our work – how to order stock, how to fill in the school's record system and so on. By contrast, there are times in our lives when we learn something about our own power – we gain new insights into ourselves and our world through critical self-awareness. In turn this may transform the way in which we see the world and the actions that we take in it. We start to think differently and so we start to act differently.

This latter kind of learning has a key place in in-service work. When we do something it is invariably linked to how we think about and see the world. Attempts to change our own or another person's behaviour often neglect the fact that the behaviour itself is embedded in a whole way of thinking, feeling and seeing which enables that person to give meaning to his or her experience. As Mezirow (1977) points out, a person's behaviour is shaped by his or her perspective. When faced with new and conflicting information we can engage in

- 'change by exception', where we tolerate the anomalies with the comforting words 'it's the exceptions that prove the rule';
- 'incremental change', where we may not even notice the changes that occur bit by bit;
- 'pendulum change', where we abandon one set of certainties for another almost without question; or
- 'paradigm change', where we reorganise what we know in a new way so that we transform our view (or perspective) of it.

Often an attempt at curriculum change actually implies 'paradigm change', but usually it results only in one of the other responses. *Real change of behaviour, as opposed to superficial or short-term changes, are often the result of a change in perspective (or paradigm), they rarely happen without it.*

When I review my own career as a teacher, I can identify, in particular, two fundamental changes to my practice in the classroom. The first concerned my approach to reading, the second concerned my approach to mathematics. No doubt there were other changes which occurred by a series of transitions, but, for these two, I feel there was an almost sudden insight . . . I had the stimulus of a course concerning the reading, but nothing remotely like that concerning the maths – although over the years I had attended several maths courses . . . In each case, I had *not* received a prescription for classroom practice but had been excited by an image of what might be possible. Until this time I had not even been able to *see* the possibility of a different type of behaviour in the classroom, let alone *do* anything about it. I was, I suppose, trapped in a cultural myth about what constituted 'reading' or 'mathematics'.

Such myths are developed by our past experience as pupils and as teachers, and control our outlook. As a result, we ourselves give rise to the dilemma implied by R.D. Laing's poem (1970):

He does not think there is anything the matter with him
because
one of the things that is
the matter with him
is that he does not think there is anything

the matter with him
therefore
we have to help him realize that,
the fact that he does not think there is anything
the matter with him
is one of the things that is
the matter with him.

What does constitute our view of reading?

If teaching is about survival then it is also about denial. We filter out peripheral information, which in itself is a useful short-term strategy for limiting stress, but in doing so we may deny facts and feelings. Although this is a human and natural response, it can give rise to tension, fear and conflict. These are, if you like, transformations trying to happen. Avoidance may just build up further long-term troubles for ourselves. An alternative is to transform our stress by paying attention to it and by trying to articulate what we know but perhaps cannot name. This reflection can help us to transform our perspective – and the liberating effect of a new perspective can be exciting.

the problem of children copying chunks of information out of books during project work – constantly discussed in the staffroom but seemingly an inevitable part of classroom life – was redefined in my mind and I could see a way into tackling it.

Such changes are typified by a process of:

● reflecting upon present practice;
● challenging familiar assumptions that influence what we do;
● exploring new ways of acting in accord with how we now see the reality of the classroom.

What Really Makes an Impact?

Conscious decisions like this to alter classroom practice take a considerable amount of time and energy to become thoroughly worked into the ebb and flow of classroom life. It can feel, however, rather like changing to a higher gear. Perhaps this also helps to explain why you cannot really change other people, nor can they change you; people can only change themselves. The best that anyone can do is to provide a structure which helps others to change, if that is what they want to do.

Activity 40: tackle individually

Review your own learning as a teacher.

(1) Choose one example which you feel made a real impact upon your practice as a teacher.
(2) Note down why you think it made such an impact.
(3) Choose one example which you feel made little or no real impact upon your practice as a teacher.
(4) Note down why you think it made so little impact.

Activity 41: tackle with one other person who has done activity 40

---

(1) Take it in turn to share the results of activity 40.
(2) Together, consider the *main differences* between the learning that made a real impact upon your practice and that which made little or no real impact.

Activity 42: tackle with three other colleagues who have tackled activities 40 and 41

---

(1) Consider whether, from your own experiences, there are things which tend to characterise learning that makes a real impact upon practice.
(2) Make a list of the things agreed by the group.
(3) Consider whether, from your own experiences, there are things which tend to characterise learning that makes little impact upon practice.
(4) Make a list of the things agreed by the group.

Activity 43: tackle as a group

---

(1) Compare the lists produced for activity 42 by each group.
(2) Discuss what implications there may be for your school-centred in-service work.

When Professional Learning Means Personal Change

This chapter has focused upon how adults learn and what that might mean for professional learning. Often such professional learning implies a reorganisation of how we see things, a transformation in our perspective. If we do experience such a qualitative change in our thinking then we are also likely to experience personal change. In Chapter 9 the activities are designed to help you consider further the images of ourselves that we hold, how they are formed and how these might help or hinder personal change.

9 PERSONAL LEARNING

Learning about Ourselves

We all develop an idea of who we are; in fact, doing so is a complicated process which extends throughout our lives. We may become acutely aware of it during 'identity' or 'life' crises, but the process itself is always part of our interaction with the world. Sometimes, particularly in adolescence, we take evidence from outside ourselves. So, although we may become increasingly able to reflect on this evidence, to some extent our view of ourselves is a social creation. In that sense, an individual is not 'context-free' in his or her ability to change – a theme further explored in Section 4, 'Change and Others' – but self-awareness is a prerequisite for really being able to change.

The purpose of this chapter is to help you consider how pressure for change can impinge upon a individual and, as a consequence, how you may be better prepared to cope with it.

The Complexity of Ourselves

> There are times when I look over the various parts of my character with perplexity. I recognize that I am made up of several persons and that the person that at the moment has the upper hand will inevitably give place to another. But which is the real one? All of them or none? (Somerset Maugham)

What we do *isn't* what we are, it is only part of us. There is a set of things that we do when we are being ourselves. Other people observe these ways in which we behave, to them that is us, let's call it Set A

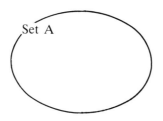

Set A

On the other hand, there is also a set of things that *we* recognise and accept as ourselves. This is how we see ourselves, our self-image, let's call it set B. The trouble is that although these two sets overlap, like this

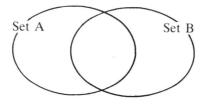

they are very rarely *congruent* so that they exactly correspond. That is not all, for what really makes each of us who we are, is an unknown area, unknown to ourselves and to others. There has to be if there is such a thing as growth. We are all changing all the time, that is what life is about. We grow or we atrophy. So the picture looks more like this:

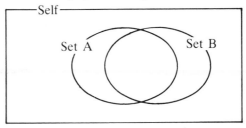

This image helps to provide a model for exploring our knowledge of ourselves and our relations with others.

(1) *Our public display*. This is the part of ourself that we know about and which others see. On the diagram, it would be the shaded section.

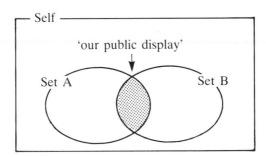

In the various situations in which we act out our lives, there are often certain expectations of us – and we conform to them.

(2) *Our blind spot*. This is the part of ourself that others see, but which we don't know about. On the diagram, it would be the shaded section.

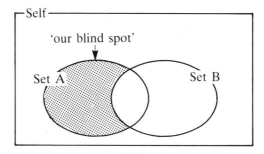

There may be a considerable mismatch between our perception of ourselves and the perceptions of others.

There may be a considerable mismatch . . .

As Robert Burns put it:

> O wad some Pow'r the gifties gie us
> To see oursels as others see us
> It wad frae many a blunder free us,
> And foolish notion

This gift can be given to us, but it relies on feedback from others – and that implies honesty and trust, with ourselves and with others.

(3) *Our dreamer spot.* This is the part of ourself that we know but no one else does. On the diagram, it would be the shaded section:

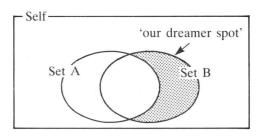

It contains our fears, our fantasies and our thrills. This is our secret castle where, the heroic figure in shining armour, we wait for the right moment to show the world that we were not put on this earth in vain. All we need is a bit more luck and the right opportunities. Secrets are precious – we know that or we would share them willy-nilly – and we protect those things that are precious. Perhaps that helps to explain why it is the emotions – not the intellect – which are the basis of life. It also explains why in Chapter 1 reference is made to the foundations of personal and interpersonal change necessary for effective curriculum change. If, for example, someone appears to be hostile or threatening or critical of something we do, we may react in two ways:

(a) we may not recognise or accept that we do it in the first place. In other words whatever it is that we do is not in Set B of the diagram; or (b) we may recognise that we do it but not feel inclined to change it or adjust it. In other words, it *is* in Set B of the diagram but, for that very reason, we see it bound inextricably with our 'dreamer spot' which the other person can't even see. If our secret castle is threatened, we want to defend it – and the more we feel threatened, the greater the defences. As far as the other person is concerned, we cease to listen.

No wonder the 'hero-innovator' is likely to run into difficulties. Unless we intend to adopt medieval tactics of siege and storming, the only access to that castle is by invitation, that is, through self-disclosure. Furthermore, we may well be viewing that other castle from the safety of our own castle.
(4) *Our untapped reservoir*. This is the part of oneself that is genuinely unknown. On the diagram it would be the shaded section

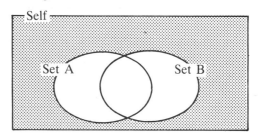

Herein lies that vast human potential which we don't even know about. During the traumatic crises of life – major illness, divorce, death of a loved one or redundancy – we are forced to question and reappraise the existing structure, to search for new possibilities in ourselves and our world and rebuild our lives. At times like that we draw on that hitherto unknown source – or go to (or up) the wall.

Activity 44: tackle individually

During your life, circumstances may have provided you with new knowledge about yourself in some of the areas discussed above.

(1) Try to find one incident for each of three areas – your 'blind spot', your 'dreamer spot' and your 'untapped reservoir'.
(2) Describe each incident briefly.
(3) Explain how each incident increased your knowledge about yourself.

The Social Construction of Ourselves

It would be naive not to acknowledge that we all exist in a social and historical context. It is this that makes each of us the unique person that we are – and it is this that presents us with both opportunities and constraints. Ideally, of course, how others see us and how we see ourselves would be one and the same. In the terms of the diagram, Set A and Set B would be congruent, like this:

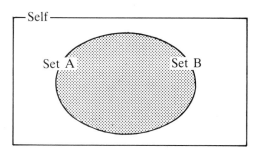

Maybe that is something towards which each of us should work; perhaps we should actively seek to increase the area of overlap in the diagram from this:

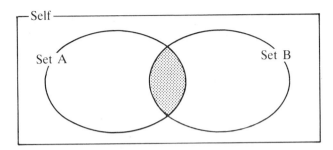

to this:

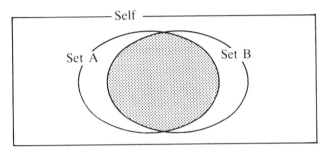

which represents a better matching of our awareness with our experience.

If this were to happen, life might become less complicated. The less internal conflicts we experience, the less external conflicts we are likely to encounter. The more at ease we are with ourselves, the more we may be at ease with others. The more honest we are to ourselves, the more honest we may be to others. The more sincere we are to ourselves, the more sincere we may be to others.

The movement towards such an ideal state depends upon the extent to which both self-disclosure and feedback are used in our interactions with other people. This, in turn, depends on us valuing ourselves and accepting other people – and that, in part, depends on whether other people seem to value and accept us. The impact of the social reflection of others upon our self-image does mean that it is possible for us to get caught up in a cyclical process, although it is usually only the 'vicious circle' of personal despair and social rejection which we recognise as happening. Cooley (1964) uses the term 'the looking-glass self' to refer to the person's self-image which is formed on the basis of perceiving how others react to him or her. The effect upon any individual of honest feedback based upon an unexpected perception can be shattering. No doubt we can all identify with the scene Cooley describes:

> The self that is most important is a reflection, largely, from the minds of others . . . We live on, cheerful, self-confident . . . until in some rude hour we learn that we do not stand as well as we thought we did, that the image of us is tarnished . . . we find with a chill of terror that

the world is cold and strange, and our self-esteem, self-confidence, and hope, being chiefly founded upon the opinions attributed to others, go down in the crash . . .

So we need to take care with others, and we want them to take care with us. A 'thinking school' has to grow out of a 'caring school'.

Activity 45: tackle individually

---

(1) For *each* member of your staff, make a rating for how *you think* they perceive you in terms of:

(a) Your performance as a professional (*not* in terms of your status in the formal hierarchy of the school);
(b) Whether they like or dislike you as a person.

Make each rating on a ten-point scale where 1 is 'not much' and 10 is 'very'. For example, you might rate Mr Smith thus:

(i) Concerning his perception of my 'professional performance', 8.
(ii) Concerning whether he likes me or not as a person, 2.

This would mean that although Mr Smith thinks that you are worthy of respect as a teacher – he doesn't like you!
(2) Plot each member of staff on a diagram, similar to the one below:

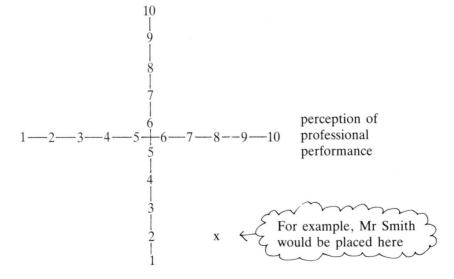

perception of whether liked

(3) Examine the pattern that emerged on your diagram. Explain why you think the pattern is as it is.

Confronting Ourselves

Some of our ideas about things external to us are inextricably linked with our self-concept. A proposal for change may threaten or contradict these ideas and, in so doing, threaten our self-concept. The urge to maintain a consistent self-image is so strong that we tend to deny, ignore or manipulate evidence in order to eliminate contradictions. However, it is often the unintentional changes which reveal contradictions and confront certain things that we believe about ourselves. All the effects of a curriculum change are not felt straight away, and may be hard to imagine when the decision to change is taken. Indeed, those implications of a curriculum change which take time to emerge may be the very ones that are important in the long run. If a proposal for change unwittingly (or wittingly) comes into conflict with our implicit 'theory of action', then it brings into question our 'survival kit'; that is, the concepts and categories that we have evolved for organising our experiences.

We all have such a conceptual system and we use it in order to understand our world. It helps us to be effective in that world and helps us to evaluate that some states of affairs are better than others. In that sense, then, these conceptual systems are not just intellectual exercises but have value attached to them. We are all operating within such a framework established and modified in the light of our experience. Our behaviour is shaped by it and is an experiment to test its predictive validity. This means that to understand someone's behaviour we need to try to understand what framework they are using to interpret the world. Equally, if we want to understand ourselves better, then we need to make our own implicit 'theories of action' explicit.

Activity 46: tackle individually

---

(1) Write the name of each member of your INSET group including yourself on a separate small card. It is helpful to have about 8-10 cards, so you can include some other names if necessary.
(2) Shuffle your cards and choose three cards at random.
(3) Consider the people whose names are on the three chosen cards. Try to sort them so that you can pair two people who are alike in some way but different from the third person. For example, 'gives constructive comment'.

(4) Now ask yourself 'What is the opposite of the characteristic perceived in the pair?' Check to ensure that your answer:

(a) is not ambiguous, e.g. 'does not give constructive comment' could mean either 'gives no comment' or 'gives destructive comment';
(b) gives the possibility of indicating intermediate gradations;
(c) does not implicitly involve different dimensions, e.g. 'Friendly – Repellent' (which involves 'Friendly – Hostile' and 'Attractive – Repellent');
(d) is not implicitly evaluative, e.g. 'loquacious – taciturn'.

(5) When you are satisfied with your characteristic, draw a matrix on a sheet of paper and write the characteristic and its opposite on the left hand side, e.g.

Characteristics	
'gives constructive comment – gives destructive comment'	

(6) Now repeat steps (2), (3), (4) and (5) (above) until you have about 12 characteristics on your matrix.
(7) Having completed the 'characteristics' section, now write the names of each member of your INSET group [together with any other names you included] on the matrix, e.g.

Characteristics	Ann	Bill	Clive	Diane	Edward	Frances
'gives constructive comment – gives destructive comment'						

(8) Take each characteristic in turn and rate each person according to that dimension. Use a scale in which 5 is high (or towards the characteristic) and 1 is low (or towards the opposite of that characteristic), e.g.

Characteristics	Ann	Bill	Clive	Diane	Edward	Frances
'gives constructive comment – gives destructive comment'	2	5	1	5	3	4

(9) When your matrix is complete, cut off and destroy the top line containing each person's name.
(10) Examine your matrix carefully. Does it highlight any patterns or issues concerning the framework within which *you* operate in this particular arena? Write brief notes to describe any insights you have gained.

Activity 47: tackle with one other person who has done activity 46

(1) Ensuring that the names have been removed, swop completed matrices.
(2) Examine your partner's matrix. What patterns or issues concerning his or her framework can you discern? Make brief notes.
(3) Now share your own notes from activity 46, part 10, and from (2) above, with your partner, and ask him or her to share their notes from activity 46, part 10, and from (2) above, with you.
(4) Describe any insights revealed by this activity.

From Knowledge to Action

This chapter has concentrated upon helping you to step out of the stream of daily experience and stop to reflect upon it. Understanding ourselves and our own constructs can help us to undergo effective change if we want to. To try to change our own behaviour we can try to see things in different ways, to create alternative constructs for interpreting the world.

If we cannot create such constructs, we can try borrowing some. The great value of other people can be the interpretative lenses they give us for looking at familiar phenomena in new ways. In Chapter 10 the activities are designed to help *you* begin making any changes of your own that you now want to try.

10 TRANSFORMING PROFESSIONAL REALITIES

Being Practical

Suppose that we do want to bring about some changes in our lives, what can we do? For each of us the answer will be dependent both on the external circumstances and our internal awareness. Merely wishing to change is not enough; it involves no real commitment, but deals with the problem at fantasy level. Instead, we have to set ourselves small, specific, realistic targets so that achieving them helps us to move away from the negative aspect of our life towards more positive aspects. In doing so, we build up our confidence in the possibility of change. The purpose of this chapter is to help you to begin this change process in practice. The activities help you to assess yourself as a professional, and as a result to determine specific change-events as targets. Of course, these in themselves may trigger a complex chain of unintentional change which, as yet, you cannot foresee. In other words, as a result of the change-events you may come to qualitatively different ways of seeing your experiences past and present.

Self-appraisal

There has been growing interest in staff appraisal during recent years, and an increasing body of literature on the subject is becoming available.

Staff-appraisal schemes are concerned with some regular and objective form of staff review. Clearly such review-and-appraisal schemes may have their place within the accountability perspective. When it comes to the exploration of mutual professional problems with colleagues, however, a more informal self-appraisal seems more appropriate. School-centred INSET can both highlight issues and create learning opportunities. There *may* be times when a school staff has a responsibility to consider those issues, but only individual teachers can utilise learning opportunities. Self-appraisal is one way in which we can review our own professional development and begin considering what steps might aid that development.

Activity 48: tackle individually

---

(1) What do you consider to be your key activities as a teacher? Try to list them in order of importance.

(2) Do you anticipate any significant changes in any of these activities during the next year or so? If so, try to specify them.

(3) What aspects of your work give you the most problems at present. Try to list them in order of importance.

(4) Consider and note what, if any, were the reasons preventing you from coping with these aspects to your own satisfaction.

(5) Are there any areas where you feel that the school could make better use of your experience and talents? If so, try to note what those areas are and what you think that you have to offer.

(6) What extra help or guidance do you feel you need to:

    (a) meet the challenge of changes mentioned in (2);
    (b) deal with the problems mentioned in (3);
    (c) help you to use your experience and talents in the context of this school?

(7) Which of these approaches would be most relevant to you? Indicate the order of priority by ranking from 1 to 6, 1 being the most relevant:

    (a) Secondment for a course at an HFE Institution.
    (b) Short LEA courses on specific issues.
    (c) Visits to other schools.
    (d) Reading.
    (e) School-based workshops/meetings.
    (f) Working alongside a colleague.

Controlling Your Experience

Self-assessment may lead us to decide to make some sort of change. Perhaps we may begin by thinking such things as 'I wish I could . . .', 'I wish I was . . .' or 'I wish I had . . .'. The next step is to try to convert this wish into a tangible course of action – if you like, a 'target for change'. Often we choose a small thing to aim for – such as leaving our desk tidy at the end of the day – simply because we know that we have a reasonable chance of actually doing it. What matters is that we feel in control over our interaction with at least one aspect of our experience.

Activity 49: tackle individually

Draw up a list of three 'targets for change' starting with a very simple one and finishing with the most difficult, e.g.

- leaving the staffroom on time at the end of break;
- tidying my desk at the end of the day;
- making time to listen to people who want to talk.

Activity 50: tackle with one other person

(1) Describe your three 'targets for change'.
(2) Ask the other person to suggest ways in which the minimum change in each area could be achieved.

Activity 51: tackle individually

Review your work for activities 49 and 50, and select a 'target for change' that you are prepared to set yourself. In relation to this change, write brief answers to the following:

- What do I need to do?
- What am I willing to do?
- Whom can I ask for help?
- Whom do I trust to measure my progress?

Other People Can Help You

The activities in this section are intended to help you respond positively to situations which may require you to learn. The process of self-appraisal, change and real learning can be eased – and indeed helped – by other people. That aspect of change is further considered in Section 4, 'Change and Others'.

SECTION FOUR
CHANGE AND OTHERS

"*Oh Lord, did you see that? I trod on a crack in the lino.*"

About This Section

The pressures associated with change may lead to stress (either personal or collective) and possibly conflict. The reactions of those involved will be many and various. Some will attend to their stress, confronting it, and in doing so begin to reappraise their world. Others will seek strategies for avoiding the stress, indeed denying it. Some of the possible implications of changing the curriculum for any individual are explored in Section 3, 'Change and You'. There it was noted that the process of significant personal change can be helped by access to the alternative ways of seeing reality offered by other people. However, the mere physical proximity of people with different perspectives does not necessarily mean that this process will take place, they could instead argue, abuse or 'cold-shoulder' each other. For a start, as we value our own ways – our 'survival kit' – so we defend them when they are threatened by information and experiences which would cause them to change or break down. Secondly, the very behaviours that we exhibit when we are acting defensively are precisely those with which other people find difficulty in coping.

The purpose of this section is to help you cope with other people in this situation. It begins by looking at those aspects which are probably the most difficult – denial and conflict – before moving on to consider how support may be provided, communications increased and the effectiveness of group life improved.

11 HANDLING DENIAL

The Discomfort That Leads to Denial

Examining and re-evaluating our existing patterns of behaviour as teachers can be very challenging. It can also be very discomforting. It may be that the process of curriculum review and development raises problems and generates experiences which are not resolved sufficiently for an individual; the past seems unsatisfactory, the future seems uncertain, perhaps forbidding, and the present seems to underline professional and personal inadequacy. The loss of confidence and self-esteem that this implies can make a person feel helpless, unable to cope with the problems he or she faces and impotent in relation to constructing a way forward. If a person has a problem then he or she must also believe that it can be resolved by personal effort, and the individual must have some self-respect. Otherwise defence mechanisms begin to be invoked – and denial is one of these.

Avoiding or denying the stress associated with change is a very human reaction; long-established practices and images provide the comfort of predictability. The main reason for trying to help someone in this position is to increase their repertoire of ways of handling his or her professional life; in particular breaking out of stereotyped patterns. In other words, it is not about stopping someone doing something, because that then removes a choice, but rather about helping that person to realise that there are additional choices and that it is possible to act on the basis of this increased range of choices.

It is not always easy to identify those who are experiencing discomfort. Obviously it helps to generate an atmosphere where people feel free to express what is troubling them – but that is only part of the story. Everything we do together involves such things as talking, listening, reading, writing and thinking. In doing so we use words or other symbols. That does not, however, guarantee that we communicate effectively. Getting through to people isn't just about overcoming barriers caused by the way we use words. Such barriers are trivial compared with those caused by the way we feel. We use words not only to convey ideas but also to protect ourselves and our self-esteem, and even to disguise the fact that we have no ideas to convey on an occasion when we are supposed to have.

It may be helpful, therefore, to begin by distinguishing in our

interactions between the words actually used and the real message behind the words. For example, how often are the words 'with all due respect' transmitted in any other way than really to mean 'without any respect at all'; or when do people say 'Can't you take a joke?' without a malicious smile? We might, then, see our communication as consisting of both dimensions; like this:

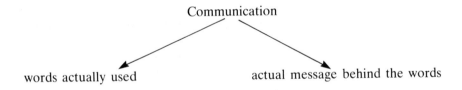

If both those dimensions are consistent in what they communicate, then perhaps we can get through to the other person. Sometimes, however, that real message stays locked within us, engaged in some sort of *internal dialogue* related to our fantasies, imaginings, beliefs and values. It is rooted in our feelings and is a reflection of inner experience. Recalling a painful memory, for example, might involve the internal dialogue. So we choose our words carefully, and the other person may never know how we really feel whilst we churn quietly inside.

At other times the dialogue may be *external*, revealing itself in communication to other people through gestures, voice tone and other non-verbal means. We might say that we have 'leaked' the real message to other people through our fingers, feet or, most importantly, our eyes, for the latter could be called 'the windows of the soul'. So it is that we intuitively respond, or fail to respond, to the non-verbal messages as well as the more verbal ones.

The purpose of this chapter is to help you examine how people try to avoid stress and change so that you might learn how to handle 'denial' constructively.

Games as a Substitute for Communication

The only mind in the world over which we have even a semblance of control is our own. We don't even know what is going on in someone else's mind yet alone have power to control it. We can listen to what another person says and we can observe that person's behaviour. On the basis of that, we can guess what might be going on in his or her mind. But if we don't like what we think is going on, the only mind we can change is our own. This may cause us to change our behaviour in the hope that the other person will notice something different and so change his or her mind.

The initiative, and the responsibility for communication, has to lie with us. If we can recognise what sort of things make us defensive, perhaps we can try to stop defending ourselves and try to avoid behaving in ways that cause others to be defensive. If we want to avoid confronting the realities of our 'blind spot' or rationalise our activities so that our self-concept remains undented, we might play games with ourselves and with others. If we resort to such tactics, then surely so must others. If we can recognise this, perhaps we can consciously adjust our own behaviour to try and prevent such blocks to communication.

What, then, we all often do as we live out our lives, is to substitute what might be called 'games' for genuine communication. The extent to which we do this tends to depend on the context, so that whilst we may communicate with some people, we may just play games with others. This idea that people tend to play certain games in their interpersonal relationships lends itself to the world of staffrooms.

Activity 52: tackle individually

In Appendix IX, p. 186, there is a list of eight games compiled for educators.

(1) Read the Appendix, 'Games Educators Play'.
(2) Consider which of these games you have played and the context in which each occurred.
(3) Select one particular incident from your own experience that seems to illustrate clearly one of the games. Describe it briefly.
(4) Analyse what you think was really happening during the game.

Activity 53: tackle with a colleague who has also done activity 52

---

(1) Share the results of activity 52.
(2) Consider the context within which those particular games were played. What characteristics did they seem to have in common?

Depending upon how we see ourselves and other people within a given context, will depend the stance that we adopt and, as a result, the type of interaction between us. In other words, how we see ourselves and others in any situation will depend on the quality of our communication – or the extent of our 'games'. Some people make us feel good – the relationship thrives on mutual respect and acceptance. Other people have the opposite effect, and the relationship deteriorates even further. It is not just the other person but what *we* are when we are with him or her that determines the success of the interaction – or otherwise.

Confronting Denial

Why do we let ourselves get into the position of 'playing games' with some people? More importantly, how can we get out of it? Unfortunately there are no easy answers. The trouble is that we can all spot everyone else's games and give them advice about how to stop it. Doing the same thing to and for ourselves is a very different matter. It requires both introspection and hardwork – and we all know plenty of techniques for avoiding both of those!

Activity 54: tackle individually

---

(1) Review your notes for activity 52.
(2) In relation to the incident described in part (3) of that activity, ask yourself:

● What did I feel?
● What did I think?
● What did I think the person was thinking about me?
● What did I think the person wanted from me?
● What did I feel about him or her?
● What did I do?
● What did I really want to do?

Other people can help us to confront our avoidance strategies and we can help them confront theirs. For example, the 'If It Weren't for Them' game described in Appendix IX, p. 187, is based upon imagining artificial constraints. The person involved imagines artificial constraints as a basis for believing that changes cannot be made. 'The parents would never agree to it' being a fairly typical response. Now of course it may be true that the parents would never agree, but that avoidance strategy can be confronted with responses such as 'How do you know?' or 'How could you persuade them?'

'Game playing' or denial and avoidance depends very heavily on stereotyped patterns of handling or responding to situations. Helping someone to confront his or her denial is often about helping that person to be more specific. Sometimes we hold on to vague generalisations as a way of stopping ourselves exercising new choices. Often when we are encouraged to be more specific we find that perhaps our problem is more manageable and that some positive thinking begins to emerge. In Appendix X, 'Confronting Avoidance', pp. 188-90, some more of these strategies such as 'rambling', 'creating catastrophies' and 'rigid expectations' are described, together with possible ideas for confronting them. The list is neither definitive nor prescriptive, the important point is for you to develop ways of helping yourself and others break out of stereotyped patterns and explore other possibilities.

Activity 55: tackle individually

---

(1) Review your work for activity 54.
(2) Read Appendix X, 'Confronting Avoidance'.
(3) Try to decide:

(a) which avoidance strategy was at work in the particular incident described, and
(b) how it might have been confronted.

Activity 56: tackle with a colleague who has also done activity 55

---

(1) Share the results of activity 55.
(2) Work through the other avoidance strategies listed in Appendix X. For each strategy ask yourselves:

(a) Has a similar thing ever happened to me and what did I do then?
(b) How else might I have handled it?

New Rules for Old Games

'Game-like' communications rest upon an illusion of certainty which, at the same time, does not bring anything more than a transient satisfaction. Acknowledging that these interactions bring only a caricature of security, rather than security itself, encourages us to experiment with new ways of handling those interactions. In turn this can transform those communications, helping them to move forward rather than recycle the same patterns. It may, of course, mean that on the way we have to face up to and resolve certain conflicts. Facing up to one's own denial, however, is an integral part of resolving external conflicts.

12 RESOLVING CONFLICT

From the General to the Particular

Conflict as an issue has already been explored at a general level in Chapter 2, 'Curriculum Change, Co-operation and Conflict'. This chapter returns to the theme at a more practical level with the purpose of providing some tangible ways of trying to resolve particular conflicts. If you are to *use* this chapter (rather than just read it) you will find it hard work and probably very emotionally draining. The only consolation is that, in the long run, unresolved conflict is even more draining.

Reviewing Your Own Perception of the Conflict

There is an old maxim that peace *within* must precede a durable peace *without*. The way we think about and see things – our conceptual systems – is, in a sense, the most important survival equipment we have. On the other hand, most of us have internal conflicts between the various ideas, beliefs and wishes we hold. Personal growth and development relies upon our continuing efforts to understand and master both ourselves and our world. Sometimes, then, we need to resolve these internal tensions for ourselves before we can adequately resolve some of our external conflicts. Often in order to do either of these we need to improve our relationships with others.

Many of the activities in Section 3, 'Change and You', and Section 4, 'Change and Others', are intended to help you do this. Whether or not you intend to proceed through this chapter now, do try to find time to reflect upon your own perspectives of the world and your relationships with your colleagues.

Activity 57: tackle individually

Consider the particular conflict concerning you at the moment.

(1) Write a brief description of the conflict as you see it.
(2) Write down a statement about the motivations and goals of your opponent. Use the format of a table as below, and put your statement in the first column.

Statement about the motivations and goals of my opponent	Reasons for supporting this view	Why I believe this

(3) Now ask yourself why you hold this view. Think of as many reasons as you can. Write these in the second column of your table.

(4) Read through your comments in the first and second columns of the table. Ask yourself 'Why do I believe this?' about each one. Write your answers in the third column.

(5) Read what you have written in the third column, ask yourself 'Do I have evidence to support this assumption?'

(6) Re-read the description of the conflict that you wrote for (1) (above). Add any further comment that you now feel is appropriate.

Using a 'Third Party'

A third party often encourages conflict resolution because his or her presence helps participants to confront one another and their problems openly. Without such a person, there may be such a backlog of hostility, fear or mistrust that any activity requiring a reorientation in the definitions of the situation and the other party will be doomed. A third party can:

(1) improve communication between parties by increasing both its openness and its accuracy. The mere act of translating, articulating and summarising one party's remarks for the other enables the checking of invalid assumptions by publicly comparing the meaning given with the meaning received.

(2) regulate what happens between the parties. Conflict resolution seems to require a number of stages based upon sequences of paired phases. These phases are of:

  ● 'differentiation' (when each participant is putting his or her own case and/or views), and

● 'integration' or the discovery of similarities between the participants.

Both of these phases need space; a third party can ensure this by shifting discussion from one phase to another.
(3) help the participants to diagnose the conflict.

Ideally such a person would have some knowledge of how to create the sort of climate within which this conflict resolution might take place and little power over those involved.
NOTE: *For the following activities (58 and 59) to have any chance of success, both parties need to recognise that:*

● *any conflict exists;*
● *there is a need to resolve the conflict.*

If either of these conditions is not met, both parties need to reflect not only on their own feelings but also on why the other party has responded in that manner.

Activity 58: you and the person with whom you are in conflict need to do this activity together

---

Discuss whom you both might accept as a third party for conflict resolution. If you decide not to involve a third party, decide how you will now proceed to resolve your conflict.

Activity 59: you and the person with whom you are in conflict need to do this activity in the presence of a third party

---

(1) Openly identify areas of mutual concern and salient issues for further exploration.
(2) Consider mutually advantageous courses of action. Since these may not be immediately apparent begin by asking each other questions of the 'What would you do if . . .?' type.
(3) Identify the course of action to be taken.

Resolving Through Re-framing

Chapter 2 attempted to help you transform your view of conflict in the context of curriculum work. This chapter has tried to offer practical help for coping with this difficult aspect of interpersonal relations. The activities have endeavoured to point out one way forward in relation to some conflicts.

Other conflicts may need a different approach more on the model of those suggested in 'The Myth of the Hero-innovator and Alternative Strategies for Organisational Change' (Appendix II). You may find that you need to return to both the ideas and the activities more than once before they really work for you. Conflict resolution, however, is so fundamental a part of all aspects of our life that it is worth the effort to achieve.

13 SUPPORTING CHANGE

The Conundrum of Professional Learning

One difficulty about in-service programmes purporting to be based on 'needs analysis' concerns *who is defining the 'needs' for whom*. There is a conventional wisdom which sees in-service work as being designed by 'task analysis' and 'needs assessment'. In other words, the task to be accomplished is analysed in terms of specific behaviours to be acquired. This determines the educational objectives for the programme in relation to what the participants need to learn. The programme itself then consists of the component skills being learned by the participant. There is nothing wrong with this approach when it is applied to some types of learning, but that, as you may have seen in Section 3, 'Change and You', is only a small part of professional learning. It is when such an approach is applied to these other types of learning that it seems ineffectual.

This has important implications for all those involved in changing, or proposing to change, the curriculum. It is further complicated by the fact that although *our own* felt needs may be the beginning point for most of us, as adults, engaging in an educational process, sometimes that process causes us to challenge the taken-for-granted assumptions which account for those felt needs.

This does, however, present a conundrum. Our learning may have little real meaning if someone else defines our needs for us, but defining our own needs is difficult and we may need to learn in order to do so. What we have to do, then, is to start from current problems, concerns and levels of understanding (otherwise we might not even start) – but that does not mean that we will, or should, end there; nor does it mean that we will not require the help and support of someone else during the process. As we experience change there are times when all of us feel the need for the help and support of someone else. At times like that we turn to, or find, someone who we feel will be able to help us in a particular learning endeavour.

Supporting change is not easy. Some of us, like some children, may have an expectation that we should be 'told' things (a 'learned helplessness' formed by such factors as past experience and current expectation). Indeed, when teachers are participants in their own learning problems often do arise, because either their confidence in their ability to exercise independent judgement or their inquiry skills remain under-

'I'm telling you straight headmaster . . . we're all together on this one and the only way you'll win is by throwing one of your usual tantrums and we all back down. . . .'

developed. Inevitably then, if someone turns to you for help you will need to decide how to handle that request. Do you stand back, do you adopt the 'rabbit-out-of-the-hat' approach to INSET (marvel at my magic!) or what do you do? The purpose of this chapter is to help you avoid the trap of providing 'unwanted answers to unasked questions' and instead make appropriate decisions about supporting a colleague, or several colleagues, during change.

Invitations to Change

In essence, it is very difficult to enforce real change and not necessarily much easier to promote it! Of course, stories abound of headteachers who have had classroom doors removed in order to encourage 'open' teaching, and others who have withdrawn supplies of crepe paper to prevent it being used in non-creative ways! But how effective are such actions in reality?

Activity 60: tackle individually

---

(1) Read the article 'The Three Year Itch' by Angela Anning (Appendix XI, pp. 191-3).
(2) Consider whether you have ever experienced a comparable phenomenon.

Schools and classrooms are active, bustling places, where a teacher is constantly receiving different signals of one sort or another. Ideas and suggestions about curriculum review and development have to compete with playground duties, marking, lesson preparation and 1,001 other things that go on in a school day from policing corridors to nursing the sick! In such situations different people give different priorities to the many facets of professional life (of which 'professional learning' may be seen as just one). This is not to say that they do not care or work hard – far from it – it merely reflects the many pressures of teaching.

Is it, then, really such a surprise that proposals for change quickly run into the ground? Most of us have both a psychological and a cultural preference for stability; and yet change (and its attendant learning) involves unpredictability and risk. Perhaps it is more surprising that other people are surprised by reactions to the process of change!

Activity 61: tackle individually

Reflect upon one specific example of a proposal for change which involved you.

(1) Briefly describe the proposal for change.
(2) Consider how you responded to the proposal for change.
(3) *After* identifying your response, consider and write down the reasons for this response.
(4) Review the reasons listed in (3) above. Ask yourself:

● Are they connected with how the invitation to change was initiated at the time?
● Are there other, more personal factors to be considered?

Make a note of your answers.
YOU WILL NEED TO TAKE THE RESULTS OF THIS ACTIVITY TO A GROUP MEETING

Activity 62: tackle as a group

---

(1) Share your results from activity 61.
(2) Consider the reasons given for the various responses. Attempt to classify them into:

● those concerned with what the respondent *knew* about the subject matter of the change proposal, i.e. cognitive reasons;
● those concerned with the respondent's *willingness* to consider the subject matter of the change proposal, i.e. the conative reasons;

● those concerned with the respondent's *feelings* when the change proposal was made, i.e. the affective reasons.

It would be foolhardy to underestimate the amount of anger, tension, bitterness and sense of exclusion that can exist among members of staff in schools involved in change. At the very outset of a school staff, or group of colleagues within a school, trying to tackle their own problems, the whole process can be helped or hindered by the way people feel about what is happening and the types of support they receive.

The Need for Help and Support

Clearly, all those involved in educational change must be concerned with the manner as well as the matter of change. Many programmes of school-centred INSET are based on a myth: that one can simply sit down with others, work out policies, aims, strategies, etc., and implement them according to rational procedures based on apparently rational agreements. Yet these take no account of the personalities of those involved, nor the effects on them of their involvement in the process of change. There may, for example, be conflicts over values, power and practicalities.

Often curriculum-development work implicitly questions our self-image. When this is the case, the affective relationship is of prime importance if such concerns as anxiety, status and identity are to be taken into account. This affective area is rarely made explicit, yet the attitudes of each person involved are clearly crucial to the success of not only the process of change but also the relationships between those involved. How are we each perceived? Are we seen as an authority or a threat? Does our colleague see us as a helper during his or her process of change or a judge with alien values? The answers to these questions will to a large extent depend on the interpersonal relationships which we each form with our colleagues.

Approaches to Support

We often become involved in a colleague's professional development with the intention of being helpful – but are we always a help? Why do some of our interventions seem to have the opposite effect from that intended? So far, this chapter seems to have put much emphasis on the pitfalls that may beset us – although this is not as negative an approach as it may seem at first. We can only ever proceed by trial and error, but that path can be less painful if we really operate the 'trial-and-error procedure' by analysing information gleaned from preceding trials to improve the next.

Activity 63: tackle individually

---

(1) Think back to one particular incident when you were given support during change.
(2) Briefly describe the incident and the circumstances surrounding it.
(3) Consider those aspects that you found helpful and those that you did not find helpful.
YOU WILL NEED TO TAKE THE RESULTS OF THIS ACTIVITY TO A GROUP MEETING

Activity 64: tackle as a group

---

(1) Share your results from activity 63.
(2) Consider what actions seem to provide helpful support for people during change.

Support through Communication

If someone tries to change us the chances are that we will resent it and resist. If they learn to live with us to try to discover our purpose, perhaps both of us will change for the better. In order to do this we must both communicate – and this will be more than simply exchanging ideas or letting us unburden ourselves. It will be encouraging a deeper exploration of issues and problems through helping us to clarify what we are saying, a support that fosters our independence rather than our dependence. In Chapter 14 the activities are designed to help you consider further your communication with colleagues and how it might be improved.

14 IMPROVING COMMUNICATION

Communication for Growth

In Chapter 13 it was suggested that the type of support offered to someone could certainly ease the process of personal change. In essence, it requires honesty, empathy and genuine communication – and if that type of support is not already on offer, perhaps everyone in the school should consider trying to ensure that it is. The activities in this chapter are intended to help you develop effective communication with colleagues so that support may be sought and given through self-disclosure and feedback.

"Lack of communication? Don't talk to me about lack of communication."

We need the help of others to develop and maintain our respect for ourselves and for other people. If we can do that we are better able to cope with change. The amount and type of feedback we receive from others is crucial to this. We sense this intuitively and use it to guide us in our search for support. We tend to talk about people being warm towards us or cold towards us, accepting or rejecting, caring or uncaring – we all mean the same thing. We know the people who help us grow – and those that don't. This aspect of interaction between people is described by Steiner (1974) in his story 'A Fuzzytale'.

Activity 65: tackle individually

In Appendix XII pp. 194-6 you will find Steiner's story about interaction.

(1) Read Appendix XII, 'A Fuzzytale'.
(2) Describe one 'Warm Fuzzy' and one 'Cold Prickly' that people have given you.

Activity 66: tackle with a colleague who has also done activity 65

Share your descriptions from activity 65.

Constructive Feedback

An important element of support is the use of constructive feedback. Feedback can be destructive when it is given only to hurt or to express hostility without any intention of improving the communication between those involved. On the other hand, it is useful when it:

● describes what someone is doing rather than placing a value on that behaviour;
● is specific rather than general;
● is directed towards something which the recipient can do something about;
● is well-timed;
● is asked for rather than imposed.

In other words, the communication between people is honest, but takes into consideration the needs of the person on the receiving end. It is worth spending some time thinking of how you set about providing such feedback.

Activity 67: tackle with one colleague whom you know well

On your own

(1) Decide what would be the most useful positive and negative feedback statements to give to your colleague.
(2) Consider how to state the feedback so it will be very clear, direct and useful to the recipient.

(3) Prepare two statements for your colleague, e.g.

'The most valuable behaviour that you exhibit in our curriculum group is the way you summarise the discussion at various stages.' 'The most negative behaviour that you exhibit in the group is the way you sometimes rummage through your briefcase when someone else is talking.'

With your colleague

(4) Share your feedback reports *verbally* with each other.

On your own

(5) Consider how you feel about the feedback received.
(6) Make a note of any ideas that you have for presenting feedback.

With your colleague

(7) Compare notes from (6) above.
(8) Suggest some practical hints for giving feedback.

YOU WILL NEED TO TAKE THE RESULTS OF THIS ACTIVITY TO A GROUP MEETING

Activity 68: tackle as a group

(1) Share your results from part 8 of activity 67.
(2) Construct a list of practical suggestions for giving feedback.

Self-disclosure

Many of us are not good listeners, especially to ourselves. Sometimes someone else can help us hear what we are actually saying, and that in itself can act as a catalyst to our thinking. Self-disclosure not only lets another person know what is going on inside us, it lets us know.

Activity 69: tackle with a colleague

(1) There are two roles, talker and listener, for this activity. You should both have the same amount of time (e.g. 30 minutes) exercising each of these roles.
(2) Decide who will be talker for the first half of the period (e.g. 30 minutes).

(3) The *talker* has to describe his or her particular problems or difficulties, e.g. what has happened, what he or she felt about it and so on.

(4) The *listener* has to make sure that he or she understands the talker *and* that the talker is understanding the meaning of what he or she is saying. This means:

- not giving advice or guidance;
- not putting interpretations on what the talker is saying;
- not recalling anecdotes from your own experience, *but* feeding back what the talker is saying only to help the talker be clear.

(5) After the talker's time is up (e.g. 30 minutes), change roles.

Getting the Message

In this chapter the focus has been on the process of communication; finding ways of communicating not just words but also the real message behind the words. The feedback we give to and receive from others can improve our communication. Unfortunately, too often we engage in the type of games people play as described in Chapter 11. Real communication is candid and honest, and is concerned with genuine understanding and the sharing of feelings and experiences. It is also extremely hard work, but it can improve our interpersonal relationships, and thereby support those personal journeys of change which may accompany any curriculum change.

In Chapter 15, the activities are designed to help you consider further the content of communication; in particular, learning through discussion.

15 LEARNING THROUGH DISCUSSION

Making Discussions Work for You

Meanings are in people, not in the words they use. Learning through discussion is an important part of the experience of each participant in any in-service work, so it is important to make the most of it. People vary enormously in the amount they like to contribute to a discussion. People are different, have different kinds of things to contribute, may speak a lot at one point and be silent at another. Some people talk a lot because they are nervous or feel that if they don't no one else will fill up the empty silences. Others stay silent because they lack confidence or prefer not to respond too quickly. Some people just prefer to listen and get a lot out of that – this too needs to be respected and they should not be pushed.

Whatever our own personal style happens to be, we all seem to expect that talking with others helps us learn, but *how* exactly? We all have

Support may be an unspoken, or even unconsidered part of a relationship

112

memories both of excellent discussions in which we have been involved –
and of desultory, useless discussions. What is it that distinguishes the two,
and how is it that we can help make a discussion what we want it to be? It
is common for us to attribute the success or failure of a discussion group
to others – especially to the leader of the group – but we seldom
acknowledge the responsibility (and the power) we have individually to
influence the usefulness of a discussion.

The purpose of this chapter is to draw on your own experiences of
valuable and valueless discussions in order to help you try and
understand:

● how these differences come about, and
● what can be done to bring about the sort of discussions you find useful.

A Basic Difficulty of Group Discussions

One of the intrinsic problems of group discussions is the number of
demands made on the participant. Each group member is involved
simultaneously in:

● listening to the discussions; ·
● thinking about what has been said and formulating points of his or her
own;
● finding suitable entry points for his or her contributions;
● attempting to maintain an overall picture of where the discussion is
heading (and if necessary intervening to change its direction).

Under this pressure, and because discussions tend to gain rapid
momentum in unexpected directions, participants often forget points they
had originally intended to make. A very narrow perspective on an issue is
frequently drawn by one or perhaps two participants and, although
several alternative points of view could have been contributed by other
group members, the process of following the thoughts of the dominant
ones drives these alternative views to the back of the minds of the other
members, or makes the views seem irrelevant in the light of the
perspective which has been imposed. Indeed, many of the less confident
participants are only too ready to believe that they have nothing relevant
to contribute to the discussion.

Characteristics of Good and Bad Discussions

Activity 70: tackle individually

---

(1) Think back to a discussion you have had fairly recently which you found exciting, useful or interesting. It might be an informal chat, or an organised meeting. Ask yourself *why* it was good? Note down a few characteristics of that discussion.
(2) Now think back to a discussion which bored you, or left you disinterested or annoyed – that you did *not* learn from. Note down a few things about why it was poor.

Activity 71: tackle with one colleague who has done activity 70

---

(1) Spend about ten minutes recounting your experiences as described in activity 70 to each other.
(2) Consider whether you find the same sorts of discussion valuable.

Activity 72: tackle with your colleague from activity 71 and two other colleagues who have tackled activity 71

---

(1) Consider:

   ● what sort of things seem to characterise good and poor discussions; and
   ● how do they come about?

(2) Make a 2-column list.

Good discussions	Poor discussions

YOU WILL NEED TO TAKE THE RESULTS OF THIS ACTIVITY TO A GROUP MEETING

Activity 73: tackle as a group

(1) Review your notes from activity 72.

(2) Each group of four should, in turn, make one point about good or poor discussions. As each point is made, consider whether everyone agrees with it.

(3) When your list seems quite comprehensive consider how you might help give rise to each good characteristic, and avoid each poor characteristic.

A Structured Approach to Discussion

You may have noticed that this chapter has been structured so that you worked in the following sequence:

- as an individual;
- in pairs;
- in small groups;
- in a large group (or plenary).

Many people find this approach to be successful because

(a) *Individual work* helps to:

- focus on the overall purpose of the discussion;
- remind participants that they each have their own points to make.

(b) *Work in pairs.* Many participants, although they may speak in a larger group, are actually very nervous when they do so, and are careful to conceal any views on which they think they might be attacked. Others become increasingly tense as they wait for an opportunity to speak until they eventually lose all confidence in the possible value of their ideas.

Talking in pairs:

- eliminates the 'public speaking' element of discussion groups and reduces the members' understandable tendency to 'paper over the cracks' in their understanding of the subject matter. A one-to-one discussion is quite different in its psychological implications from any larger group. As soon as the group size is raised to three there is the possibility of one person being 'wrong', or in other words, outweighted by numbers. Also it is harder for a shy participant to pursue a theme, since the others may take the discussion in a different direction. In fact it is easy for the shy person to revert to his or her usual 'safe' role as 'one of the quiet ones' or 'one of the less knowledgeable ones'.

● virtually compels even the shyest participant to speak, if only in response at first to the ideas of the other. Furthermore, the more dominant group members become aware that their partners have not contributed and may spontaneously attempt to elicit their ideas. In this way the less vocal participants gain confidence through practice in articulating their ideas and in many instances through receiving support for them. Indeed, this stage of discussion can be revealing both to the less forceful people in finding that their ideas are acceptable to another, and to the more vocal ones in finding that the quieter group members have more to offer than is often apparent.

● has the advantage of involving everyone immediately from the beginning of the session, and of creating a buzz of conversation so that the atmosphere of the room is one of activity and exchange of ideas rather than of awkward silences.

(c) *Working in small groups* can lead to considerable productive discussion. Ideally, it involves pairings of the existing pairs, but where overall numbers do not permit this, groups of five or six might be formed. As a result of the increase in group size the discussion will tend to be more free-ranging than in the pairs, but, in contrast with the usual group situation:

● the more nervous participants have the support of a partner in expressing the points they have agreed between them. Having tried an idea out and having found that at least one other person is willing to support it, greatly increases the confidence of the shyer group members. Where the group contains only four members there is the added advantage that neither pairs can be 'outnumbered';

● it is quite large enough to generate a wide range of ideas and is small enough to give all members an opportunity to speak. Where several of these small groups are working in the same room there is the additional benefit that the room is seldom silent so that gaps in the discussion are not so noticeable. Indeed, a group member may overhear a useful new theme from one of the other groups.

(d) *Working in a large group*. The final stage of bringing small groups together for a general reporting session may mean that there are too many participants for a free discussion. However, it does:

● give a purpose to the earlier discussion;
● allow the different groups to become aware of aspects of the topic which they have left uncovered;
● foster cohesiveness within the whole group.

The chairperson can help to make coherent sense of the various contributions by making notes of points on a blackboard and summarising at the end. (Taking one point from each group in turn tends to be fairer in terms of time allocation than dealing with the entire report from one group before moving to the next.)

Overcoming Difficulties of Discussion

By now you have probably got plenty of ideas of your own for helping discussion along. It is useful always to bear in mind the dimension of 'concrete-abstract' in relation to discussions. Abstractions, of course, are vitally necessary, but they are often not the most effective vehicle for discussions. By making discussion concrete, relating it to actual, practical experience some of the difficulties which lead to casual chat or confused debate may be avoided. 'Chatting', in itself, is important. It can mean that you are sharing your experiences, gaining insight from other people's ideas or getting support for what you do. Any group of teachers contains a great deal of educational expertise and 'chatting' is one way in which this may be accessed. However, in order for the whole group to benefit, rather than individuals on an *ad hoc* basis, it may be helpful to:

(a) Focus on a particular issue or activity and look at it in terms of your own experience.
(b) Respond to another person's concrete statements about what they do and what they feel by searching your personal experience for similar situations or feelings.
   This can be more supportive than a question which can feel like an inquisition or a criticism. You may not intend your question to be received in that way, but if the other person feels put on the spot, he or she may become isolated. At the same time, do remember that there is also a fine line separating supportive statements of this nature from those which turn the occasion into egocentric anecdote swapping!
(c) Try to monitor what you are saying. If you are beginning sentences with phrases like: 'I think . . .', 'I believe . . .', 'My view is . . .', 'In my opinion . . .' 'Most people think . . .' it's likely you are talking in an abstract or theoretical manner. Try to re-state your thoughts as statements about your own experiences and feelings.

These three points have been found useful by other people for developing exploratory discussion. Underpinning them all is the need for people not to be afraid to talk openly. People do fear that they may be laughed at or criticised for the ideas or feelings they put forward. The following activity can help to create a less critical atmosphere.

Activity 74: tackle as a group

---

(1) Think of one of your beliefs or views or values about a particular issue, e.g.
'My belief: that children should have a positive attitude towards mathematics.'
(2) Look back over your actions of the past week or month and find an example of where your actions contradict your belief, e.g.
'My action: I made Peter stay in at playtime to do extra sums because he had misbehaved.'
(3) Write your contradictory belief and action on a piece of paper, fold it up and put it in a hat along with everyone else's pieces of paper.
(4) Mix around the folded pieces of paper and get everyone to draw one piece of paper out.
(5) Go around the group so that each person reads out what is on his or her paper.

Beyond Discussions

Everyone has internal conflicts with contradictory beliefs and actions; and usually they do not live up to their own expectations. By creating both a climate in which people feel able to express themselves honestly and a structure through which this may be done people can learn considerably from each other.

So far, you have considered the need for genuine communication in the context of supporting others during change. This in itself is hard work with only two people involved, so aren't the difficulties which can arise between two individuals compounded when several people try to talk and work together as a group? Well, as we all know, they are. Many groups *are* ineffective, but *you* can contribute to improving the quality of group life. In Chapter 16 the activities are designed to help you do this.

16 WORKING IN GROUPS

Group Life

Any consideration of a group and its behaviour has to take account of the individuals involved and the expectations and beliefs they bring to the situation. But groups of all sizes, rather like individuals, develop their own 'identities' and behave at both conscious and unconscious levels. So groups come to develop attitudes and beliefs about themselves – and about others – and these are determined not only by the rational discussions and decisions taken within the group but also by the beliefs and assumptions on which the group work.

Being a member of a group can be very stimulating – or very frustrating. Invariably, much curriculum development and in-service work takes place in groups. The purpose of this chapter is to help you to examine some ways of making the in-service activity a positive experience for *all* members of your group.

Making Your Group More Effective

Activity 75: tackle individually

---

(1) Consider three groups to which you have belonged at some stage in your career. List them as A, B and C in the matrix below.
(2) Now take each group in turn and rate it against the criteria listed in the matrix. Use a rating system of 1-6 (where 6 means 'meets the criterion very well').
(3) Now consider the following questions:

  ● Was the group with the highest rating also the most successful in your own experience?
  ● What had contributed to the most successful group working so well?
  ● How could the least successful of the groups be improved?

(4) List what implications, if any, your work for this activity has for your current in-service work.

Group selected

Criteria	A_____	B_____	C_____
Participants shared a clear concept of the purpose of the group			
The group was effective at getting things done			
There were close personal relationships within the group			
Participants felt a strong sense of personal commitment to the group			
Total rating			

YOU WILL NEED TO TAKE THE RESULTS OF THIS ACTIVITY TO A GROUP MEETING

A considerable amount has been written about groups and how they work. In your context, what matters is the 'knowledge for doing' rather than the 'knowledge about', and an essential way of getting access to this type of knowledge is to reflect upon your own direct experience. For example, when you reflect upon the group that scored highly on the criterion 'there were close personal relationships within the group' for activity 75, you might decide that this was because:

● disagreement was not taken as personal rejection by people in the group;
● everyone felt accepted and liked by the others;
● people trusted each other;
● everyone's contribution was taken seriously, valued and respected.

Just as this begins to give you some pointers towards what to do in a group, so an examination of the performance of an unsuccessful group can warn you of the pitfalls to avoid. For example, the group scoring very low on the criterion 'participants felt a strong sense of personal commitment to the group', might, upon reflection, have manifested symptoms such as:

● only a few members of the group participated; the rest seemed to withdraw mentally;
● some people felt misunderstood or ignored;
● some people felt no responsibility for, or commitment to, the decision.

Activity 76: tackle individually

(1) Review your work for activity 75.
(2) For each criterion listed in activity 75, e.g. 'participants shared a clear concept of the purpose of the group',

   (a) consider the group that scored highest against that rating;
   (b) ask yourself why you hold this view. Think of as many reasons as you can;
   (c) consider the group that scored lowest against that rating;
   (d) ask yourself why you hold this view. Think of as many reasons as you can.

(3) Write down your responses in a table, e.g.

Criteria	Reasons for meeting this criterion well	Reasons for not meeting this criterion well
Participants shared a clear concept of the purpose of the group	Underlying assumptions were brought out into the open and discussed	The issue was implicitly defined as a 'win-lose' situation

(4) Make a list of some things that you might actually do to improve the functioning of your present group. Try to phrase each item not as an abstraction but as a specific action.

YOU WILL NEED TO TAKE THE RESULTS OF THIS ACTIVITY TO A GROUP MEETING

Activity 77: tackle as a group

Share your results from part (4), activity 75, and part (4), activity 76.

Coping with the Practicalities

Group meetings can be greatly helped or hindered by very practical things such as appropriate furniture and equipment for the job that needs to be done, information circulated, the records kept etc. Warwick (1982) suggests the following questions as a checklist:

- what is the purpose of the meeting?
- is a meeting appropriate?
- how should it be planned?
- who will attend?
- what preparation do they need?
- how shall prior information be presented?
- where shall the meeting take place?
- when shall it be held?
- how shall the room be set out?

These may seem obvious, but how often have you attended meetings where these questions have not even been considered let alone adequately answered?

Activity 78: tackle as a group

In the context of the next meeting planned by the group:

(1) Review the checklist of questions above, amend them as appropriate.
(2) Consider each question, either deciding the answer on-the-spot, or delegating responsibility to a member of the group to sort it out.

The Fundamental Need for Trust

In this chapter emphasis has been on building the life of your group so that it can become an effective support system for educational change. Throughout Section 4 an important theme has been the need for trust. Without it your motives for supporting change may be questioned, your communication impaired and your discussions less productive. With it, a supportive climate can be created in which people can confront their reactions to change, learn and grow. If one of the biggest single barriers to support is a low level of trust, then it is worth remembering that trust takes a long time to achieve but can be destroyed in seconds.

SECTION FIVE
OVERVIEW

About This Section

This book has helped you to look at a number of different facets of school-centred in-service work in a practical way. By this stage you will have experienced some of the ideas and activities in action for yourself, so they will not be inert terms but meaningful elements of your own professional life. The approach has been to encourage you to:

● *experience* curriculum development with colleagues;
● *reflect* upon that experience and look for possible explanations of what happened;
● *generate your own theories* that make sense of the experience by setting explanations of what happened on a particular occasion in a particular school into a wider framework of understanding. This theory then helping to guide your future practice.

The purpose of this particular section is not to 'tie up loose ends', but to help you pause and consider for yourselves where you are now and where you might be going. Finding time both to engage in practice *and* to reflect systematically upon it is difficult. However, we believe that time invested in the latter at this stage will have enormous benefit for the former in the future.

17 SUSTAINING THE APPROACH

The Challenge for School-centred INSET

There is a widespread assumption that school-centred INSET helps to create the 'thinking school'. In other words, a school which acts as a rational, problem-solving organisation engaging in any necessary corporate professional development rather than one which reacts in a reflexive trial-and-error way. This, it is assumed, is achieved through a kind of continuous educational workshop and results in an improved educational experience for the pupils. Whilst it cannot be denied that school-centred INSET is a necessary condition of achieving this goal, it may not be sufficient.

Real learning involves taking risks, and yet most of us are creatures of safety. There are limits to rationality, and we may not even recognise those things that give rise to these limits. Our responses to problem-situations may be limited by our emotional reactions; limited by something which we think is really there but which exists only in our imagination or limited by our biases subtly imbibed from the culture in which we exist.

'Thinking schools' begin with 'reflecting' teachers; teachers who establish for themselves what are their 'limits' and how they can reach beyond them; teachers who establish an inner dialogue between the action they take and the reflections they make; teachers who establish their own 'vision' for their own practice.

Activity 79: tackle individually

---

(1) Write a description of the professional teacher you would like to be. Try to be as specific as possible.

(2) Make a checklist which would help you to review your progress towards this ideal.

(3) Choose *one* thing that is within your control and for which you are prepared periodically to review your progress towards.

The Processes of Effective School-centred INSET

In Chapter 1 you met the idea that any attempt to tackle a curriculum issue at a school-based level needs an interplay between the three elements:

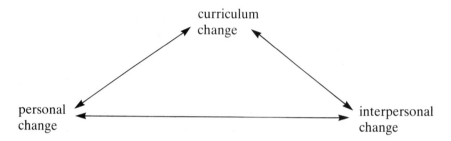

Each of these elements involves a process:

(i) *Curriculum change* is concerned with the *process* of identifying, defining and solving problems specific to the particular school.

(ii) *Personal change* is concerned with the *process* of perspective transformation – or seeing the world in new ways – which is often implicit in any real change for an individual. It necessitates:

- reflecting upon our present practice;
- challenging familiar assumptions which influence that practice;
- exploring new ways of acting in accord with how we now view reality.

(iii) *Interpersonal change* is concerned with the *process* of effective communication, so that mutual support may be sought and given through self-disclosure and feedback.

Throughout your work these three processes may have been active, although, of course, you may not have always been conscious of that. You were, however, asked to keep a diary of your responses to stage (b) (p. 12) of your group meetings – 'Reflecting upon the process of working on your particular curriculum issue or problem'. The reason for this was because it enabled you to keep your finger on 'the pulse' of your thoughts and your emotions. Your written responses, then, provide brief snapshots of what was happening to you during the whole work. Now it is time to respond to your responses.

Activity 80: tackle individually

---

(1) Review your 'responses' to group meetings with your colleagues as contained in your diary.
(2) Consider and write down

- five things you learnt about the curriculum issue itself;
- five things you learnt about group problem-solving;
- five things you learnt about effective communication;
- five things you learnt about yourself;
- five practical applications for your own teaching arising from the work.

Activity 81: tackle with one other person who has done activity 80

---

(1) Share your results from activity 80.
(2) Consider whether you learnt similar things from the work.

Activity 82: tackle with another pair of colleagues who have done activities 80 and 81

---

(1) Consider:

- what sort of things seem to characterise curriculum review and development with colleagues in your school; and
- what are their implications for further work of this kind in your school?

(2) Make a 2-column list.

Characteristics of curriculum review and development with colleagues in *this* school	Implications for further work of this kind in *this* school

Activity 83: tackle as a group

As a group
(1) Compare the lists produced for activity 82 by each sub-group.

On your own
(2) In relation to your work as a teacher, in this particular school, consider:

  (a) what your biggest anxiety is;
  (b) what your greatest wish is.

(3) Write your 'anxiety' and your 'wish' each on a separate piece of paper and fold the paper.

As a group
(4) Place your pieces of paper in two separate hats (one for 'anxieties' and one for 'wishes') and stir them round.
(5) Pass the hats around so each person can draw out one 'anxiety' and one 'wish'.
(6) In turn, read out the pieces of paper which you have drawn so that the group can:

  (a) identify who wrote it;
  (b) suggest ways of overcoming the anxiety and of gaining the wish.

(7) Decide what further action, if any, needs to be taken as a result of this meeting.

Institutionalising the Processes

Schools and their teachers are constantly receiving 'invitations' to change, from both within and outside the educational system. Often these invitations result in innovation without change. One of the reasons is because innovation is usually approached in the form of an 'organ transplant'. It neglects the situationally specific context into which it is introduced. Perhaps the process of change is more dynamic and complex. If we represent it in flow-chart form we can begin to see how the various elements may relate to each other. Instead of growing on from whatever exists within a school too often attempts are made to transplant practice from another context. Inevitably, the usual difficulties of rejection occur.

So, although it is superficially attractive to present teachers with a gift-wrapped box containing a neat definition of the problem and its solution,

> *Consider* the
> problem and
> what needs
> to be done

– it only *looks* quicker and easier. It assumes too many things, and yet the only thing that may be assumed is that all teachers, in one way or other, provide curriculum experience for pupils.

> *Provide*
> curriculum
> experience

Some teachers may share the innovator's perception of the problem so much that they find it a suitable starting point for improving the curriculum. Other teachers may define the problem in a different way or not even recognise it as a problem. Yet others, however, will not even respond to the problem, preferring to put it to one side.

> *Provide*
> curriculum
> experience

> *Consider* the
> problem and
> what needs to
> be done

Part of the difficulty is that innovators have often concentrated on the formulated products of their own thinking rather than attempting to articulate the process which led them to want to initiate change in the first place.

It may be worth trying to tease out this process as in Figure 17.1 (p. 134). Presumably it involves a decision to improve curriculum provision because there seems to be a problem needing to be tackled.

Figure 17.1

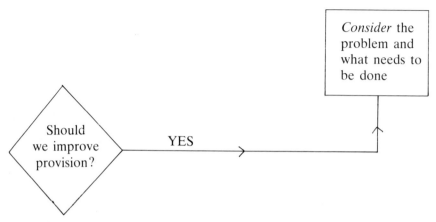

Again, presumably, this decision was taken after noticing shortcomings in what was going on at the time. In other words, engaging in some sort of evaluation of existing practice (Figure 17.2).

Figure 17.2

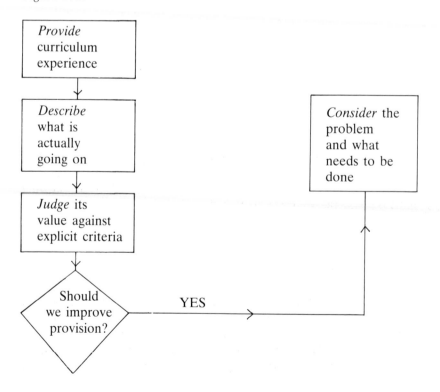

Indeed, the whole process of curriculum change might be represented by a model like Figure 17.3.

Figure 17.3

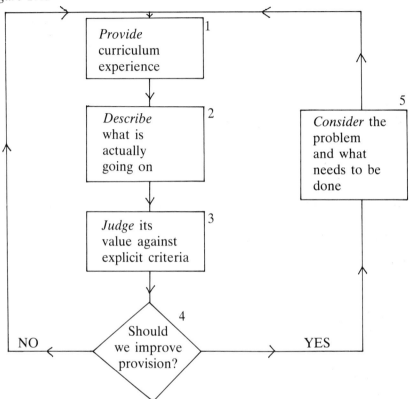

A school which is able to review its operating methods seriously and undertake activities which will improve the curriculum actually experienced by the pupils is a 'thinking' school. In practice, this means moving beyond Box 1 in the diagram so that the whole dynamic of the process becomes a conscious part of the school's life.

The Power of Teachers

Why, then, is it so difficult to get these processes of effective curriculum review and development going in a school? One answer may be that teachers do not have real control over their own learning.

The approach implied by this book was described in Section 1 as being 'about exploring mutual professional problems with colleagues', not about coercing or manipulating them. Other models of curriculum change do exist. Whilst we may easily recognise coercion at work, manipulation may be much more imperceptible. Since both are characterised by dependence, it is difficult to see how they can produce 'reflective' teachers working in 'thinking' schools. At the root, then, of the curriculum change issue is power. You may have worked through the chapter on group discussion in Section 4, 'Change and Others'. There it is mentioned that it

> is common for us to attribute the success or failure of a discussion group to others – especially to the leader of the group – but we seldom acknowledge the responsibility (and the power) we have individually to influence the usefulness of a discussion.

In that instance, what we *each* have to do is, in relation to discussions, consider how we might help give rise to any good characteristics and avoid any poor characteristics. As it is in that particular context, so too in the wider context. We all have the capacity to change our world for ourselves. Of course, we have first to be aware of this and, if we are not, then we have to learn to use our power to make such changes in our lives. Until that happens, teachers can never seriously challenge those beyond the school who actively reach into and structure the culture and experience of the INSET undertaken by those inside the school. Often the only real choice that exists is a negative one whereby a teacher can choose not to take up the INSET provision on offer. Consent, of course, is a form of power over power, but it is re-active rather than active. What happens, then, is that many teachers prefer not to engage in INSET because, although they find it difficult not to subscribe to the values of that INSET, they find it of questionable practical use for their own professional work, i.e. as was pointed out in Section 3, 'Change and You', it clashes with the values of their implicit 'theories of action'. Thus, we get what Freire calls the 'culture of silence'. Changes imposed from above, however well intended, rarely bring about real change for the individual.

So how does that process of coming to take charge of your own world and, in particular, of having real control over your own learning, come about? Much of it is to do with confidence. Confidence both to define and to resolve one's own problems. This is not quite the same as participating in 'needs-assessed' INSET, since the articulation by any one of their needs is a complex task. Indeed, it may be something that becomes possible during, or as a result of, effective professional development rather than its starting point.

There are, after all, a number of difficulties concerned with 'the identification of needs'. A stated need may be a symptom rather than a cause of problems, or it may be a diversionary tactic used because the person is afraid to be open. Some people may have a vested interest in identifying the needs of others (a form of work creation perhaps), while yet other people may genuinely not be used to identifying and stating their needs. Needs, then, have to be defined both in terms of immediate awareness *and* of understanding the cultural and psychological assumptions influencing the perception of needs. Blindly helping someone to blindly follow the dictates of an unexamined set of assumptions seems as questionable as coercing or manipulating them. What we have to do is start from that person's world as they see it with the problematic situations as they see them; but that does not mean that the person involved should not be encouraged to re-frame the problem nor to experiment to find what consequences and implications can be made to follow from it. In effect, to learn to listen when the situation talks back.

School-centred INSET is not about transmitting the values and interests of external agencies into the school, but of the school negotiating its own values and agendas for action. If a school then wishes to draw upon external agencies, it should be in order to *service* those teachers who have realised their own power and wish to create change for themselves.

In Conclusion

The course team hope that you have found working with these materials interesting and stimulating. You may remember the BBC series 'Pennies from Heaven' which was popular several years ago. It was very powerful for it illustrated so well the gap between the promise and the reality. The pedlars of dreams selling song-sheets from battered suitcases. These song-sheets being bought by eager people who saw in them the vision of a new and better world – only to wake up in the morning to find that reality is still with them and the song-sheet didn't tell them how to face the music of life.

The salesmen offered an illusion which was an escape, not a solution, but the people bought them because they were incapable of transforming their own world. They had failed to learn how to take charge of it.

We feel that this analogy can be applied to INSET. In which case, we hope that you no longer feel the need to buy the song-sheets.

SECTION SIX
GUIDE TO THE ACTIVITIES

About This Section

This section will give you some idea of both the type of work and the amount of time required by the various activities in the book. Each activity has been included under more than one descriptor, and these are listed alphabetically for ease of reference. You need to remember that:

(1) this book is not primarily intended to be an 'interesting read'. The ideas will only come alive if you do the activities;
(2) you use only the activities which you feel will be helpful to you;
(3) using the recommended format for group meetings (see pp. 9-11) will help you determine which activities will be appropriate for your circumstances;
(4) *all the activity times given are only for guidance*; some activities may take less time, some more, depending upon your colleagues and your context;
(5) the text immediately preceding an activity explains that activity in more detail;
(6) some activities form a natural sequence;
(7) some activities require you to work on your own, some require you to work with one colleague, some require you to work with a group. You can check the particular requirements for an activity in Chapter 19.

We estimate that, if you did every single activity in this book, it would take about 45-50 hours. You need to set your own priorities for choosing activities.

18 FOCUS OF EACH ACTIVITY

Focus of activity	Activity number
A	
Arguing about the curriculum	1
Avoiding change	52-3
B	
Brainstorming	15
Breaking down a problem into manageable parts	16-17
C	
Classification	16
Classroom observation and analysis	22-9
Conflict resolution	4-8, 57-9
Confronting denial	54-6
Considering the future implications of your P536 experience for your school	82-3
Counselling	69
Creating a less critical atmosphere	74
Creating your own vision	79
Curriculum debate	1
D	
Data collection	22-35
Decision-making	36
Defining a problem	13-14
Designing investigations	18-21
Different aspects of learning	38-9
Discussions	70-3
E	
Effective groups	75-7

Focus of activity   Activity number

Effective meetings   78
Exploring your own perspectives   46-7
External expertise   33-5

F

Feedback   65-8
Feelings engendered by change   60-2
Finding out more about yourself   44

G

Games educators play   52-3
Generating ideas   15

H

Handling avoidance strategies   54-6
How others may see you   45
Humour to relieve tension   74
Hypothesis-formation   18

I

Idea specification   18
Identifying and sharing concerns about the
    curriculum   9-10
Implementing solutions   37
Implicit knowledge   3
Improving group interaction   75-7
Information collection   22-35
Interaction between people   75-7

L

Learning about teaching   40-3
Learning through discussion   70-4
Learning through 'reflection-in-action'   3
Lowering tensions   4-6

Focus of activity   Activity number

M

Myth of the hero-innovator   2,8

O

Organising meetings   78

P

Personal constructs   46-7
Planning investigations   18-21
'Political' strategies for gaining influence   8
Practical ways of changing   49-50
Problem formulation   13-14
Problems of promoting change   60
Professional learning   40-3

R

Reactions of others to you   45
Reflecting upon your P536 experience   80-1
Resolving conflict   4-8, 57-9
Responding to invitations to change   61-2
Reviewing your professional life   48

S

School visits   30-2
Self-appraisal   48
Self-assessment   48
Self-disclosure   69
Self-knowledge   44
Setting up hypotheses   18
Sharing out the work   17
Starting points for sharing experiences   11-12
Supporting change   63-4

T

Targets for change   49-51
Types of adult learning   38-9

Focus of activity	Activity number
U	
Understanding how you see the world	46-7
V	
Visiting other classrooms	30-2

19 TYPES AND TIMES OF ACTIVITIES

Activity number	Page	Type of Activity	Approximate time (minutes)
1	4	Private study	15
2	7	Private study	20
3	7	Private study	5
4	18	Group work	50
5	18	Private study	10
6	19	Group work	30
7	20	Private study	15
8	20	Private study	20
9	28	Private study	30
10	28	Group work	60
11	29	Private study	30
12	29	Group work	60
13	32	Group work	30
14	33	Group work	30
15	34	Group work	30
16	35	Group work	30
17	36	Group work	30
18	40	Private study or group work	45
19	41	Private study or group work	30
20	42	Private study or group work	45
21	42	Group work	60
22	48	Individual classroom work	<60
23	48	Private study with one colleague	30
24	48	Individual classroom work	variable
25	49	Private study	90
26	49	Group work	60
27	50	Classroom work with one colleague	<60
28	50	Private study with one colleague	90
29	50	Group work	60
30	53	Private study or group work	60 plus visiting time
31	53	Private study or group work	60

Activity number	Page	Type of Activity	Approximate time (minutes)
32	53	Group work	60
33	53	Small group or whole group work	60 plus time with 'outsider'
34	54	Private study or group work	60
35	54	Group work	60
36	57	Group work	60
37	59	Group work	60
38	68	Private study	30
39	68	Group work	60
40	71	Private study	10
41	71	Work with one colleague	10
42	72	Work with three other colleagues	20
43	72	Group work	20
44	77	Private study	45
45	79	Private study	45
46	80	Private study	60
47	82	Work with one colleague	30
48	85	Private study	45
49	86	Private study	15
50	86	Work with one colleague	20
51	86	Private study	30
52	95	Private study	30
53	96	Work with one colleague	20
54	96	Private study	30
55	97	Private study	15
56	97	Work with one colleague	45
57	99	Private study	30
58	101	Work with one colleague	30
59	101	Work with two colleagues	60
60	104	Private study	15
61	105	Private study	30
62	105	Group work	30
63	107	Private study	15
64	107	Group work	60
65	109	Private study	30
66	109	Work with one colleague	10
67	109	Work with one colleague	40
68	110	Group work	60
69	110	Work with one colleague	60

Activity number	Page	Type of Activity	Approximate time (minutes)
70	114	Private study	10
71	114	Work with one colleague	10
72	114	Group work	20
73	115	Group work	30
74	118	Group work	20
75	119	Private study	45
76	121	Private study	45
77	122	Group work	60
78	122	Group work	15
79	129	Private study	45
80	131	Private study	60
81	131	Work with one colleague	30
82	131	Group work	60
83	132	Group work	60

SECTION SEVEN
APPENDICES

APPENDIX I: The Saber-tooth Curriculum
by *J. Abner Peddiwell*

The first great educational theorist and practitioner of whom my imagination has any record (began Dr Peddiwell in his best professional tone) was a man of Chellean times whose full name was New-Fist-Hammer-Maker but whom, for convenience, I shall hereafter call New-Fist.

New-Fist was a doer, in spite of the fact that there was little in his environment with which to do anything very complex. You have undoubtedly heard of the pear-shaped, chipped-stone tool which archeologists call the coup-de-poing or fist hammer. New-Fist gained his name and a considerable local prestige by producing one of these artifacts in a less rough and more useful form than any previously known to his tribe. His hunting clubs were generally superior weapons, moreover, and his fire-using techniques were patterns of simplicity and precision. He knew how to do things his community needed to have done, and he had the energy and will to go ahead and do them. By virtue of these characteristics he was an educated man.

New-Fist was also a thinker. Then, as now, there were few lengths to which men would not go to avoid the labour and pain of thought. More readily than his fellows, New-Fist pushed himself beyond those lengths to the point where cerebration was inevitable. The same quality of intelligence which led him into the socially approved activity of producing a superior artifact also led him to engage in the socially disapproved practice of thinking. When other men gorged themselves on the proceeds of a successful hunt and vegetated in dull stupor for many hours thereafter, New-Fist ate a little less heartily, slept a little less stupidly, and arose a little earlier than his comrades to sit by the fire and think. He would stare moodily at the flickering flames and wonder about various parts of his environment until he finally got to the point where he became strongly dissatisfied with the accustomed ways of his tribe. He began to catch glimpses of ways in which life might be made better for himself, his family, and his group. By virtue of this development, he became a dangerous man.

This was the background that made this doer and thinker hit upon the concept of a conscious, systematic education. The immediate stimulus which put him directly into the practice of education came from watching his children at play. He saw these children at the cave entrance before the fire engaged in activity with bones and sticks and brightly colored pebbles. He noted that they seemed to have no purpose in their play beyond immediate pleasure in the activity itself. He compared their activity with that of the grown-up members of the tribe. The children played for fun; the adults worked for security and enrichment of their lives. The children dealt with bones, sticks, and pebbles; the adults with food, shelter, and clothing. The children protected themselves from boredom; the adults protected themselves from danger.

"They are living what they learn, and learning what they live."

'If I could only get these children to do the things that will give more and better food, shelter, clothing, and security,' thought New-Fist, 'I would be helping this tribe to have a better life. When the children became grown, they would have more meat to eat, more skins to keep them warm, better caves in which to sleep, and less danger from the striped death with the curving teeth that walks these trails by night.'

Having set up an educational goal, New-Fist proceeded to construct a curriculum for reaching that goal.

'What things must we tribesmen know how to do in order to live with full bellies, warm backs, and minds free from fear?' he asked himself.

To answer this question, he ran various activities over in his mind. 'We have to catch fish with our bare hands in the pool far up the creek beyond that big bend,' he said to himself. 'We have to catch fish with our bare hands in the pool right at the bend. We have to catch them in the same way in the pool just this side of the bend. And so we catch them in the next pool and the next and the next. Always we catch them with our bare hands.'

Thus, New-Fist discovered the first subject of the first curriculum – fish-grabbing-with-the-bare-hands.

'Also we club the little woolly horses,' he continued with his analysis. 'We club them along the bank of the creek where they come down to drink. We club them in the thickets where they lie down to sleep. We club them in the upland meadow where they graze. Wherever we find them we club them.' So woolly-horse-clubbing was seen to be the second main subject in the curriculum.

'And finally, we drive away the saber-tooth tigers with fire,' New-Fist went on in his thinking. 'We drive them from the mouth of our caves with fire. We drive them from our trail with burning branches. We wave firebrands to drive them from our drinking hole. Always we have to drive them away, and always we drive them with fire.'

Thus was discovered the third subject – saber-tooth-tiger-scaring-with-fire.

Having developed a curriculum, New-Fist took his children with him as he went about his activities. He gave them an opportunity to practice these three subjects. The children liked to learn. It was more fun for them to engage in these purposeful activities than to play with colored stones just for the fun of it. They learned the new activities well, and so the educational system was a success.

As New-Fist's children grew older, it was plain to see that they had an advantage in good and safe living over other children who had never been educated systematically. Some of the more intelligent members of the tribe began to do as New-Fist had done, and the teaching of fish-grabbing, horse-clubbing, and tiger-scaring became more and more to be accepted as the heart of real education.

For a long time, however, there were certain more conservative members of the tribe who resisted the new, formal educational system on religious grounds. 'The Great Mystery who speaks in thunder and moves in lightning,' they announced impressively, 'the Great Mystery who gives men life and takes it from them as he wills – if that Great Mystery had wanted children to practice fish-grabbing, horse-clubbing, and tiger-scaring before they were grown up, he would have taught them these activities himself by implanting in their natures instincts for fish-grabbing, horse-clubbing, and tiger-scaring. New-Fist is not only impious to attempt something the Great Mystery never intended to have done; he is also a damned fool for trying to change human nature.'

Whereupon approximately half of these critics took up the solemn chant, 'If you oppose the will of the Great Mystery, you must die,' and the remainder sang derisively in unison, 'You can't change human nature.'

Being an educational statesman as well as an educational administrator and theorist, New-Fist replied politely to both arguments. To the more theologically minded, he said that, as a matter of fact, the Great Mystery had ordered this new work done, that he even did the work himself by causing children to want to learn, that children could not learn by themselves without divine aid, that they could not learn at all except through the power of the Great Mystery, and that nobody could really understand the will of the Great Mystery concerning fish, horses, and saber-tooth tigers unless he had been well grounded in the three fundamental subjects of the New-Fist school. To the human-nature-cannot-be-changed shouters, New-Fist pointed out the fact that paleolithic culture had attained its high level by changes in human nature and that it seemed almost unpatriotic to deny the very process which had made the community great.

'I know you, my fellow tribesmen,' the pioneer educator ended his argument gravely, 'I know you as humble and devoted servants of the Great Mystery. I know that you would not for one moment consciously oppose yourselves to his will. I know you as intelligent and loyal citizens of this great cave-realm, and I know that your pure and noble patriotism will not permit you to do anything which will block the development of that most cave-realmish of all our institutions – the paleolithic educational system. Now that you understand the true nature and purpose of this institution, I am serenely confident that there are no reasonable lengths to which you will not go in its defence and its support.'

By this appeal the forces of conservatism were won over to the side of the new school, and in due time everybody in the community knew that the heart of good education lay in the three subjects of fish-grabbing, horse-clubbing, and tiger-scaring. New-Fist and his contemporaries grew old and were gathered by the Great Mystery to the Land of the Sunset far down the creek. Other men followed their educational ways more and more, until at last all the children of the tribe were practiced systematically in the three fundamentals. Thus the tribe prospered and was happy in the possession of adequate meat, skins, and security.

It is to be supposed that all would have gone well forever with this good educational system if conditions of life in that community had remained forever the same. But conditions changed, and life which had once been so safe and happy in the cave-realm valley became insecure and disturbing.

A new ice age was approaching in that part of the world. A great glacier came down from the neighboring mountain range to the north. Year after year it crept closer and closer to the head-water of the creek which ran through the tribe's valley, until at length it reached the stream and began to melt into the water. Dirt and gravel which the glacier had collected on its long journey were dropped into the creek. The water grew muddy. What had once been a crystal-clear stream in which one could see easily to the bottom was now a milky stream into which one could not see at all.

At once the life of the community was changed in one very important respect. It was no longer possible to catch fish with the bare hands. The fish could not be seen in the muddy water. For some years, moreover, the fish in this creek had been getting more timid, agile, and intelligent. The stupid, clumsy, brave fish, of which originally there had been a great many, had been caught with the bare hands for fish generation after fish generation, until only fish of superior intelligence and agility were left. These smart fish, hiding in the muddy water under the newly deposited glacial boulders, eluded the hands of the most expertly trained fish-grabber. Those tribesmen who had studied advanced fish-grabbing in the secondary school could do no better than their less well-educated fellows who had taken only an elementary course in the subject, and even the university graduates with majors in ichthyology were baffled by the problem. No matter how good a man's fish-grabbing education had been, he could not grab fish when he could not find fish to grab.

The melting waters of the approaching ice sheet also made the country wetter. The ground became marshy far back from the banks of the creek. The stupid woolly horses, standing only five or six hands high and running on four-toed front feet and three-toed hind feet, although admirable objects for clubbing, had one dangerous characteristic. They were ambitious. They all wanted to learn to run on their middle toes. They all had visions of becoming powerful and aggressive animals instead of little and timid ones. They dreamed of a far-distant day when some of their descendants would be sixteen hands high, weigh more than half a ton, and be able to pitch their would-be riders into the dirt. They knew they could never attain these goals in a wet, marshy country, so they all went east to the dry, open plains, far from the paleolithic hunting grounds. Their places were taken by little antelopes who came down with the ice sheet and were so shy and speedy and had so keen a scent for danger that no one could approach them closely enough to club them.

The best-trained horse-clubbers of the tribe went out day after day and employed the most efficient techniques taught in the schools, but day after day they returned empty-handed. A horse-clubbing education of the highest types could get no results when there were no horses to club.

Finally, to complete the disruption of paleolithic life and education, the new dampness in the air gave the saber-tooth tigers pneumonia, a disease to which these animals were peculiarly susceptible and to which most of them succumbed. A few moth-eaten specimens crept south to the desert, it is true, but they were pitifully few and weak representatives of a once numerous and powerful race.

So there were no more tigers to scare in the paleolithic community, and the best tiger-scaring techniques became only academic exercises, good in themselves, perhaps, but not necessary for tribal security. Yet this danger to the people was lost only to be replaced by another and even greater danger, for with the advancing ice sheet came ferocious glacial bears which were not afraid of fire, which walked the trails by day as well as by night, and which could not be driven away by the most advanced methods developed in the tiger-scaring courses of the schools.

The community was now in a very difficult situation. There was no fish or meat for food, no hides for clothing, and no security from the hairy death that walked the trails day and night. Adjustment to this difficulty had to be made at once if the tribe was not to become extinct.

Fortunately for the tribe, however, there were men in it of the old New-Fist breed, men who had the ability to do and the daring to think. One of them stood by the muddy stream, his stomach contracting with hunger pains, longing for some way to get a fish to eat. Again and again he had tried the old fish-grabbing technique that day, hoping desperately that it might work, but now in black despair he finally rejected all that he had learned in the schools and looked about him for some new way to get fish from that stream. There were stout but slender vines hanging from trees along the bank. He pulled them down and began to fasten them together more or less aimlessly. As he worked, the vision of what he might do to satisfy his hunger and that of his crying children back in the cave grew clearer. His black despair lightened a little. He worked more rapidly and intelligently. At last he had it – a net, a crude seine. He called a companion and explained the device. The two men took the net into the water, into pool after pool, and in one hour they caught more fish – intelligent fish in muddy water – than the whole tribe could have caught in a day under the best fish-grabbing conditions.

Another intelligent member of the tribe wandered hungrily through the woods where once the stupid little horses had abounded but where now only the elusive antelope could be seen. He had tried the horse-clubbing technique on the antelope until he was fully convinced of its futility. He knew that one would starve who relied on school learning to get him meat in those woods. Thus it was that he too, like the fish-net inventor, was finally impelled by hunger to new ways. He bent a strong, springy young tree over an antelope trail, hung a noosed vine therefrom, and fastened the whole device in so ingenious a fashion that the passing animal would release a trigger and be snared neatly when the tree jerked upright. By setting a line of these snares, he was able in one night to secure more meat and skins than a dozen horse-clubbers in the old days had secured in a week.

A third tribesman, determined to meet the problem of the ferocious bears, also forgot what he had been taught in school and began to think in direct and radical fashion. Finally, as a result of this thinking, he dug a deep pit in a bear trail, covered it with branches in such a way that a bear would walk out on it unsuspectingly, fall through to the bottom, and remain trapped until the tribesmen could come up and despatch him with sticks and stones at their leisure. The inventor showed his friends how to dig and camouflage other pits until all the trails around the community were furnished with them. Thus the tribe had even more security than before and in addition had the great additional store of meat and skins which they secured from the captured bears.

As the knowledge of these new inventions spread, all the members of the tribes were engaged in familiarizing themselves with the new ways of living. Men worked hard at making fish nets, setting antelope snares, and digging bear pits. The tribe was busy and prosperous.

There were a few thoughtful men who asked questions as they worked. Some of them even criticized the schools.

'These new activities of net-making and operating, snare-setting, and pit-digging are indispensable to modern existence,' they said. 'Why can't they be taught in school?' The safe and sober majority had a quick reply to this naive question. 'School!' they snorted derisively. 'You aren't in school now. You are out here in the dirt working to preserve the life and happiness of the tribe. What have these practical activities got to do with schools? You're not saying lessons now. You'd better forget your lessons and your academic ideals of fish-grabbing, horse-clubbing, and tiger-scaring if you want to eat, keep warm, and have some measure of security from sudden death.'

The radicals persisted a little in their questioning. 'Fish-net-making and using, antelope-snare construction and operation, and bear-catching and killing,' they pointed out, 'require intelligence and skills – things we claim to develop in schools. They are also activities we need to know. Why can't the schools teach them?'

But most of the tribe, and particularly the wise old men who controlled the school, smiled indulgently at this suggestion. 'That wouldn't be education,' they said gently.

'But why wouldn't it be?' asked the radicals. 'Because it would be mere training,' explained the old men patiently. 'With all the intricate details of fish-grabbing, horse-clubbing, and tiger-scaring – the standard cultural subjects – the school curriculum is too crowded now. We can't add these fads and frills of net-making, antelope-snaring, and – of all things – bear-killing. Why, at the very thought, the body of the great New-Fist, founder of our paleolithic educational system, would turn over in its burial cairn. What we need to do is to give our young people a more thorough grounding in the fundamentals. Even the graduates of the secondary schools don't know the art of fish-grabbing in any complete sense nowadays, they swing their horse clubs awkwardly too, and as for the old science of tiger-scaring – well, even the teachers seem to lack the real flair for the subject which we oldsters got in our teens and never forgot.' 'But, damn it,' exploded one of the radicals, 'how can any person with good sense be interested in such useless activities? What is the point of trying to catch fish with the bare hands when it just can't be done any more. How can a boy learn to club horses when there are no horses left to club? And why in hell should children try to scare tigers with fire when the tigers are dead and gone?' 'Don't be foolish,' said the wise old men, smiling most kindly smiles. 'We don't teach fish-grabbing to grab fish; we teach it to develop a generalized agility which can never be developed by mere training. We don't teach horse-clubbing to club horses; we teach it to develop a generalized strength in the learner which he can never get from so prosaic and specialized a thing as antelope-snare-setting. We don't teach tiger-scaring to scare tigers; we teach it for the purpose of giving that noble courage which carries over into all the affairs of life and which can never come from so base an activity as bear-killing.'

All the radicals were silenced by this statement, all except the one who was most radical of all. He felt abashed, it is true, but he was so radical that he made one last protest.

'But – but anyway,' he suggested, 'you will have to admit that times have changed. Couldn't you please try those other more up-to-date activities? Maybe they have some educational value after all?'

Even the man's fellow radicals felt that this was going a little too far.

The wise old men were indignant. Their kindly smiles faded. 'If you had any education yourself,' they said severely, 'you would know that the essence of true education is timelessness. It is something that endures through changing conditions like a solid rock standing squarely and firmly in the middle of a raging torrent. You must know that there are some eternal verities, and the saber-tooth curriculum is one of them!'

APPENDIX II: The Myth of the Hero-innovator and Alternative
Strategies for Organisational Change
by *N. Georgiades* and *L. Phillimore*

This paper deals not with the form and content of training syllabi for personnel about to embark upon behaviour modification programmes in hospitals and community settings, but with different strategies for the implementation of innovation and change in these institutions. The first part of the paper addresses the question of whether training is the complete answer to inducing innovation and change into various settings; the second suggests some alternative strategies to accomplish the same objectives.

It would have been convenient if we could have presented a theoretical package on this topic which would have answered most if not all practical questions. However, it has been suggested that most of the theories in the field of organisational change are attempts to explain the unknowable in terms of the not worth knowing. As in most of the applied behaviourial sciences, research and theory on planned organisational change *follow* practice. This may reflect either the difficulties of doing the necessary research, or the impotence of research in creating practical theory and contributing to improved practice (cf. Friedlander and Brown 1974). Whatever the reason, we find ourselves devoid of a presentable theory, and thus will turn to the question of whether the traditional forms of training are adequate to achieving the objective of change.

Particular reference will be made to evidence of educational innovation drawn from educational research. Although it is true that the rate of change inside educational institutions has increased (for instance, in 1930 it was estimated that 15 years need to elapse before something like 3% of schools adopted a particular change, while in 1960 it was estimated that 7 years need elapse before 11% of schools adopted an innovation), it remains a fact that innovation and change in schools is slow (cf. Miles 1964). Schools are still everywhere in need of change and improvement. We believe this is due primarily to continued emphasis upon training as the predominant change strategy: training not only for newcomers to the profession but also for those who are already in schools with some experience.

The assumptions behind training as a strategy for inducing organis-ational changes are based upon the psychological fallacy that since work organisations are made up of individuals, we can change the organisation by changing its individual members. There is a plethora of evidence to refute this proposition; not only the generalised psychological research relating to the nature of resistance to change at the workplace (cf. Watson 1969), but also specific research into the evaluation of training programmes.

Morrison and McIntyre (1969), summing up the effectiveness of teacher training, said 'Almost every relevant investigation, whatever the instrument used, has found that the changes in expressed attitudes during training are followed by changes in the opposite direction during the first year of teaching.' Morrison and McIntyre (1967) had previously found that for 3-year-trained students, this reversal of attitudes far from cancelled out all the changes that occurred during the training period, but for 1-year-trained graduates the overall effect was a return to original attitudes by the end of two years on the job. They conclude: 'Changes in the direction of increased naturalism, radicalism and tender-mindedness among teachers in training are to some extent reversed as a result of full-time teaching, and this reversal is taking place within a relatively brief period after leaving the training college.'

Turning to industry we find that Fleishman (1953) reported a similar study in the International Harvester Organisation. He showed that despite first-class training of supervisory personnel the greatest influence upon how the supervisor actually behaved back home in the plant was the leadership of his immediate supervisor. Fleishman says 'an implication of these results seems to be that if the old way of doing things in the plant situation is still the shortest path to approval by the boss, then this is what the foreman really learns. Existing behaviour patterns are part of and are moulded by the culture of the work situation. In order to effectively produce changes in the foreman's behaviour some changes in his back home-in-the plant environment would also seem to be necessary. The training course alone cannot do it.'

The same point was summarised even more effectively by Katz and Kahn (1966). They say: 'The essential weakness of the individual approach to organisational change is the psychological fallacy of concentrating upon individuals without regard to the role relationships that constitute the social system of which they are part. The assumption is being made that since the organisation is made up of individuals we can change the organisation by changing those individuals. This is not so much an illogical proposition as it is an oversimplification which neglects the interrelationships of people in an organisational structure and fails to point to aspects of individual behaviour which need to be changed.'

This then is the myth of the hero-innovator: the idea that you can produce, by training, a knight in shining armour who, loins girded with new technology and beliefs, will assault his organisational fortress and institute changes both in himself and others at a stroke. Such a view is ingenuous. The fact of the matter is that organisations such as schools and hospitals will, like dragons, eat hero-innovators for breakfast.

What guidance can occupational psychology offer to ensure that such organisations receive newly trained hero-innovators without gobbling them up? We offer two general points and six specific guidelines which may be of some assistance.

THE GENERAL POINTS

1. To initiate a planned programme of change inside hospitals or community settings, the initiator must consider very carefully the question 'Who is my client?' It will become increasingly necessary for managers of planned change to cease regarding the individual patient as the client and move to a more systems-oriented view of the entire organisation in which the patient is to be treated as the client. The objective increasingly will be to move away from the one-to-one treatment relationship into the role of *organisational change agent* or manager of change. This may well mean leaving the treatment role to the newly trained experts, whether they be psychologists, nurses or teachers. The manager of change must concentrate her or his attention upon preparing the culture in which these experts are to work.

2. Secondly, and this follows from the first general point, it may be necessary to radically reappraise the time scale upon which you work. Organisational change that is to be permanent is a lengthy business, and results cannot be achieved hastily. Currently it is estimated that 3-5 years are needed for a fundamental organisational change in commercial or industrial organisations. There is no reason to believe that hospitals or schools would be any more amenable to change.

The implications of these two general points are clear. Although it is possible to initiate a special (usually called experimental) ward or teaching environment very rapidly by cutting through the bureaucratic red tape, by concentrating one's attention upon the technical competence of the personnel and the all too often glaring needs of patients, the prognosis for such units is poor. Lack of attention by the manager of the change to the needs of others in the total system, and an understandable desire for haste in order to alleviate patient conditions, may produce a situation in which the support for the experimental situation (both financial and emotional) is at best half-hearted and at worst grudging. It also follows that the manager should not necessarily regard step one of the process as the training of key personnel: what might be called the cultivation of the host culture is the primary step. Training can of course proceed concurrently. Preparing the way for trained personnel may take as long as 12 months, but to plant them in an unprepared and hostile environment may do their cause more harm than good.

THE SIX GUIDELINES

These six guidelines are intended more as a checklist or reminder rather than a comprehensive treatise. Our concern is only with the strategy of change and not the goals which the strategies might achieve. We have been strongly influenced in the preparation of these points by an unpublished paper by R. Harrison (1971) and Margulies and Wallace (1973). There are at least two major strategic goals with which these guidelines might help.

The first is to gain influence based upon the expertise and ability which you undoubtedly have rather than try to exert influence through channels of authority and power which you may or may not have, and by doing so deploy your limited economic and human resources in order to maximise your impact. The second strategic goal is to maintain your team as a team, particularly when members come up against strong effects of pressure or stress. It will be necessary for them to retain high morale as an intact group even when troubles set in.

Guideline 1

The manager of the change effort should work with the forces within the organisation which are supportive of change and improvement rather than working against those which are defensive and resistant to change. It is far better to find someone who wants to help and wants you to work with her or him than it is to try and convince sceptics that they need your assistance. Wherever possible, follow the path of the least organisational resistance to achieve your goals rather than confronting the resistance.

This guideline requires you to be sensitive to the psychological needs of those in the organisation with whom you interact, particularly to individual and group needs which promote resistance to change. The key skill in this process is the ability to listen. The guideline also implies no large-scale, across-the-board, activity: no mass training, no mass public-relations exercises. As manager of change you will probably have limited resources available to you and these are weakened and absorbed by the organisation if you attempt such full frontal attacks. The results are invariably disappointing.

Guideline 2

Try to develop what has been called a 'critical mass' in each change project. The manager of change should aim to produce a self-sustaining team of workers which is self-motivated and powered from within. The action implications of this guideline are again two-fold. First, always work on the principle of building teams (or Groups in the social psychology sense): never allow individuals to be isolated. Try and build a team of workers in a particular ward or school situation who are all committed to the same ideology and have the same level of technical skill. Never place an individual in a confronting or possibly hostile and threatening situation without the support of colleagues. Secondly, try and locate key people in the organisation through whom the team will be able to work. It may be necessary to spend some time on locating these key people and developing their interests systematically. This internal support system will help you to maintain the progress of your entire project, particularly in times of crisis.

Guideline 3

Wherever possible, the manager of change should work with the organisationally 'healthy' parts of the system which have the will and the resources to improve (for a more complete definition of organisational health see Georgiades 1972). The team should avoid being seduced or pressured into working with or for parts of the system which might be regarded as lost causes – individuals or groups in the organisation which have lost the ability to cope with the situation as it is. For instance try not to accept people to be trained as key personnel simply because the system cannot find anything else to do with 'her' or 'him' or because the individual sees your programme as a way of escaping from previous conflicts or stress. Further, try not to accept wards or classes where previous innovations have failed or where absenteeism or staff turnover is the highest. Usually, change requires *additional* energy and talent during the period of transition. Performance in change situations (however measured) worsens, even after the most beneficial changes, until everybody learns how to make the change work up to its potential. Persons or groups whose performance is sub-standard or barely adequate usually cannot afford and are not allowed the additional resources and the period of further decreased performance which is usually required to change successfully. These people are unusually defensive in their reactions to outsiders who offer help.

Guideline 4

The manager of the change team should try to work with individuals and groups who have as much freedom and discretion in managing their own operations and resources as possible. It profits little to work out an agreed change with someone who turns out not to have the authority to carry it out.

Guideline 5

This guideline is clearly linked to Guideline 4, and it concerns the level of commitment and involvement of the top management team in the change programme. The manager should try to obtain appropriate and realistic levels of involvement by key personnel in the hospital or school system. This does not mean that the highest levels of management need necessarily be totally involved in the programme. Individuals at the top level in bureaucratic organisations are often too personally identified with the *status quo* for this to be possible. Often the best supporters of innovation and change are among the ranks of people just below the top, where the personal commitment to the present is less and where the drive for achievement may be higher than at the very top. At the very minimum, however, the manager should have received *permission* for the change to occur by those in a top management position. Frequently, the unspoken qualifier in this situation is 'It's OK as long as we don't have to do anything differently.' Of course, if it is possible to enlist top management's support and encouragement so much the better, but this is frequently a much more difficult proposition.

Guideline 6

The last guideline concerns the role of the manager of the change in protecting the members of the team from undue pressure and stress. Arrangements should be made for most of the team to work in small groups or pairs for mutual learning and support. People should not be expected to work alone in highly stressful situations until they are quite experienced. Attempts should be made to prevent premature evaluation of the team's activities. The senior manager should attempt to absorb a large proportion of the pressure from above and outside himself. He should make a special effort to build strong personal support relationships amongst the unit members. Frequent group meetings should be held in order to allow the team to discuss their own anxieties and doubts about the kind of work that they are doing. Presentations and demonstrations of new techniques and processes by outsiders as well as attendance at professional meetings and courses should be built into the timetable of the team. Finally, the manager of the team will also have to assume the responsibility of not only being supportive to individual members but also of developing the kinds of relationships which will facilitate the graceful egress of those who feel that they are not making the right kind of progress or that are finding the going just too rough.

In this paper we have attempted to show that traditional forms of training, directed at producing innovation and change in hospital or community settings, tend to be inadequate. Evidence was cited from studies of education and industrial training which indicates the need to place greater emphasis upon the 'back-home' situation of the newly trained innovator. To assist managers of change to create a more appropriate organisational climate, which will facilitate and perpetuate innovation, we have suggested six guidelines. These are based broadly upon the need to obtain influences and credibility within the organisation and the needs of the innovating group to maintain high cohesion in the face of contrary organisation pressure.

The predominant emphasis has been upon the re-examination of the role of the psychologist as team leader in change projects together with a more realistic appraisal of the time scales of organisational change.

We hope that the paper represents an attempt to bridge the artificial gap which appears to exist between the work of the clinical, educational and occupational psychologists.

From: *Behaviour Modification with the Severely Retarded*, C.C. Kiernan and F. Peter Woodford (eds), Study Group 8 of the Institute for Research into Mental and Multiple Handicap, Associated Scientific Publishers, Amsterdam

References

FLEISHMAN, E.A. (1953) 'Leadership Climate, Human Relations Training and Supervisory Behaviour', *Personnel Psychol.*, 6, 205-22

FRIEDLANDER, F. and BROWN, L.D. (1974) 'Organisation Development', *Ann. Rev. Psychol.*, 25, 313-41

GEORGIADES, N.J. (1972), 'The New Organisation Men' in E. Butterworth and D. Weir (eds), *Social Problems of Modern Britain*, Fontana Collins, London

HARRISON, R. (1971), 'Strategy Guidelines for an Internal Organisation Development Unit', unpublished

KATZ, D. and KAHN, R.L. (1966) *The Social Psychology of Organisations*, Wiley, New York

MARGULIES, N. and WALLACE, J. (1973) *Organisational Change – Techniques and Applications*, Scott-Foresman, Illinois

MILES, M.B. (ed.) (1964) *Innovation in Education*, Teachers College, New York

MORRISON, A. and McINTYRE, D. (1967) 'Changes in Opinion About Education During the First Year of Teaching', *Br. J. Soc. Clin. Psychol.*, 6, 161-3

—— and —— (1969) *Teachers and Teaching*, Penguin Books, Harmondsworth, Middx

WATSON, G. (1969) 'Resistance to Change' in W.A. Bennis, K.D.

Benne and R. Chin (eds), *The Planning of Change*, 2nd edn, Holt, Rinehart & Winston, New York

APPENDIX III: Fundamental Activity for Every Group Meeting

Activity: tackle as a group

---

(1) *At the first stage of the meeting, i.e. working on the 'content'*

On your own,

    (a) Consider the question 'What do I want to get from this meeting?'
    (b) Make a note of your answer in the diary section of your work folder.

In the group,

    (c) Take it in turns to read out your notes from (b) above.
    (d) Consider and answer the question 'Which of these purposes can we agree to act upon as a group?'
    (e) Identify alternative course of action for achieving the goal agreed in (d) by answering the question 'What are the alternative ways of doing this available to us?'
    (f) Review the alternative courses of action and decide upon the particular one to follow in this meeting by answering the question 'What shall we actually do?'

(2) *At the second stage of the meeting, i.e. reflecting on the 'process'*

On your own,

    (g) Consider the question 'Can I give two examples of where we worked well together?'
    (h) Make a note of your answer in the diary section of your work folder.
    (i) Consider the question 'Can I give two examples which lead me to think that we can improve our performance?'
    (j) Make a note of your answer in the diary section of your work folder.
    (k) Consider the question 'What have I learnt about school-centred curriculum development today?'

(l)   Make a note of your answer in the diary section of your work folder.

In the group,

(m) Take it in turns to read out your notes from (h), (j) and (l) above. No one should comment upon what is said.

(3) *At the third stage of the meeting i.e. deciding future activity*

As a group,

(n) Review

- the possible themes outlined in the 'Contents pages' and Section 6, 'Guide to the Activities'; and
- the comments expressed in (m) above.

(o) Consider and decide what to do:

(i) at the next meeting;
(ii) inbetween meetings;

by answering the question 'What action can we take to improve what we are doing?'

YOU WILL NEED TO KEEP THE RESULTS OF THIS ACTIVITY

APPENDIX IV: 'Scoring Points'

One member of your group will need to act as 'organiser', helping with the scoring and the time-keeping. Everyone else should participate in the activity.

Materials Needed

● 1 set of instructions per participant. See pp. 173-4.
● 1 pen or pencil per participant.

Seating Plan

There should be enough space for two groups to meet separately without interrupting or disrupting each other. In between there should be two chairs for group representatives, these should be facing each other, e.g.

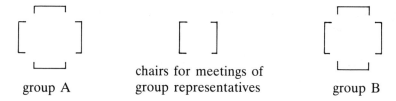

group A   chairs for meetings of group representatives   group B

Numbers

Participants should be divided into two teams and named either group A or group B.

How to Begin and Run Rounds

(1) A group can only communicate with the other group in any way, verbally or non-verbally, when told to do so by the organiser.
(2) Give out an instruction sheet to each participant. Members of a group should teach each other WHAT TO DO. The organiser should allow

about 3-5 minutes of teaching and learning and not answer any questions.
(3) The rules are:

(a) The activity involves 10 rounds of choice.
(b) In each round a group makes a choice of either X or Y.
(c) Each round is scored; a group's score is based on the choice of the other group in addition to their own.
THE ORGANISER SHOULD GO THROUGH THE SCORING MATRIX.
(d) There are special bonus rounds where it is possible to score extra points. Before a group makes its choice for one of these rounds, a representative of the group can confer with a representative of the other group.
(e) Groups can only talk when they are discussing and making their choice. Once the X or Y has been put down, no talking.

(4) Do round (1). Ensure that each group hears and understands the scoring.
(5) Proceed through the rounds. Ensure that during 'bonus rounds', groups do not make their choice or mark their sheets until *after discussing the outcome* of the representatives meeting.

IF YOU HAVE ATTENDED AN INTER-SCHOOL COURSE BASED ON P536, YOU MAY HAVE PLAYED AND BE FAMILIAR WITH 'Win As Much As You Can'. EITHER 'Scoring Points' OR 'Win As Much As You Can' ARE APPROPRIATE FOR THIS ACTIVITY.

'Scoring Points'

Directions

For ten successive rounds your group (A or B) will choose either an 'X' or a 'Y'. The 'pay off' for each round is dependent upon the choices made by both.

Both choose	X :	each group loses 3 points
Both choose	Y :	each group wins 3 points
A chooses B chooses	X : Y :	A wins 6 points B loses 6 points
A chooses B chooses	Y : X :	A loses 6 points B wins 6 points

Strategy

You are to confer in your group and make a JOINT DECISION. Before rounds 4, 9 and 10 representatives from each group meet and talk prior to the groups making their own choice. The 'pay-off' for these rounds is increased.

'Scoring Points'

Round	Strategy		Choice X Y		Pay off		Cumulative points
	Time allowed (mins)	Confer with			Points won	Points lost	
1	3	own group					
2	2	own group					
3	2	own group					
4 (Bonus round)	3	one group rep. from each group			Bonus: pay-off is multiplied by 2		
	2	own group					
5	$1\frac{1}{2}$	own group					
6	$1\frac{1}{2}$	own group					
7	$1\frac{1}{2}$	own group					
8	2	own group					
9 (Bonus round)	3	one group rep. from each group			Bonus: pay-off is multiplied by 6		
	5	own group					
10 (Bonus round)	3	one group rep. from each group			Bonus: pay-off is multiplied by 10		
	5	own group					

On Friday morning Andrew arrived early for the lesson and stationed himself by the teacher's desk, determined to get some information before he did anything else. While he was waiting, he looked round the room to see if there were any survivors from the last lesson and decided that there were at least three people that he had seen before: Jeanette Butler, the boy in the pink shirt and another boy whose appearance worried Andrew because he was sure there was something wrong with him. He was hideously swollen about the body but very thin in the face. Andrew leaned against the desk and wondered what kind of disease could possibly cause a person to become such a horrid shape. The boy's spindly legs seemed hardly strong enough to support the rest of him.

'You're the new boy, are you?' said someone beside him. 'I'm Miss Beale, who are you?'

'I'm Mitchell', said Andrew. 'Andrew Mitchell, Miss.' It sounded like a silly sort of tongue twister.

'How do you like it here?' said Miss Beale. Andrew didn't intend to be side-tracked.

'What are we supposed to be doing?' he asked.

'That rather depends on you', said Miss Beale. 'In General Studies you can choose your own subject and follow it through. You'll be rather behind the others but you can start on a project now and work on it through the holidays. That's what most of the others will do, if they haven't finished by next week.'

Andrew found this hard to believe.

'What are you interested in?' asked Miss Beale.

'Motor racing, guinea pigs,' said Andrew.

'Well, either of those would do for a start,' said Miss Beale. 'Perhaps Victor would show you round so that you can see how the others set about it.' Andrew thought she wanted to be rid of him and when he turned round he found that a restive queue had formed behind him. Miss Beale directed him to Victor. He was the very fat boy with the very thin face.

Andrew was reluctant to go any closer. How could he stroll up and hold a normal conversation with anyone so deformed? He picked up his satchel and walked casually round the fat boy's desk as though he just happened to be passing it. When he got close, Andrew realized that

Victor was not fat at all. On the contrary, he was exceptionally thin; all of him, not just his head and legs. The fat part was made up of clothes. Andrew could see a white T-shirt, a red shirt, a blue sweater and a red sweater. Further down he wore a pair of black jeans with orange patches sewn over the knees and yellow patches on the hip pockets. Over it all he had an anorak so covered in badges and buttons that it was difficult to tell what colour it was.

In fact, he was not so much dressed as camouflaged. Even his hair seemed to be some part of a disguise, more like a wig than live hair, dusty black as if it had been kicked round the floor before being put on. It was so long at the front that Victor was actually looking through it. His ears stuck out cheerfully, like a Radar device.

'Miss Beale said you would show me round, to look at the projects,' said Andrew.

'Why, do you want to copy one?' asked Victor, lifting a strand of hair and exposing one eye. 'You could copy mine, only someone might recognize it. I've done that three times already.'

'Whatever for?' said Andrew. 'Don't you get tired of it?'

Victor shook his head and his hair.

'That's only once a year. I did that two times at the junior school and now I'm doing that again,' he said. 'I do fish, every time. Fish are easy. They're all the same shape.'

'No, they're not,' said Andrew.

'They are when I do them,' said Victor. He spun his book round, with one finger, to show Andrew the drawings. His fish were not only all the same shape, they were all the same shape as slugs. Underneath each drawing was a printed heading: BRAEM: TENSH: CARP: STIKLBAK: SHARK. It was the only way of telling them apart. The shark and bream were identical, except that the shark had a row of teeth like tank traps.

'Isn't there a "c" in stickleback?' said Andrew. Victor looked at his work.

'You're right.' He crossed out both 'k's, substituted 'c's and pushed the book away, the better to study it. 'I got that wrong last year.'

Andrew flipped over a few pages. There were more slugs: PLACE: COD: SAWFISH: and a stringy thing with a frill round its neck: EEL.

'Don't you have to write anything?' asked Andrew.

'Yes, look. I wrote a bit back here. About every four pages will do,' said Victor. 'Miss Beale, she keeps saying I ought to write more but she's glad when I don't. She's got to read it. Nobody can read my writing.' Andrew was not surprised. Victor's writing was a sort of code to deceive the enemy, with punctuation marks in unlikely places to confuse anyone who came too close to cracking the code. He watched Andrew counting the full stops in one sentence and said, 'I put those in while I think about the next word. I like doing question marks better.' He pointed out two or three specimens, independent question marks, without questions. They looked like curled feathers out of a pillow. One had a face.

'Do you put a question mark in every sentence?' said Andrew.

'Oh, yes. I know you don't actually need them,' said Victor, 'but they're nice to do.'

Andrew turned to the last page of the book. There was a drawing of a whale.

'Whales aren't fish,' said Andrew.

'Aren't they?' said Victor. 'Are you sure? I always put a whale in.'

'Whales are mammals.'

'What's a mammal?' said Victor. He wrote 'This is. not a fish?' under his whale and closed the book. 'Come and see the others.'

'Mammals don't lay eggs,' said Andrew, as they set off round the room.

'That's a pity,' said Victor. 'I'd like to see a whale's egg. Big as a bath, wouldn't that be?' He stopped by the boy in the pink shirt. 'Let's have a look at your project, Tim.'

Andrew thought he had seen most of Tim's project before. It featured a man in a tree, knotty with muscles and wearing a leopard skin.

'Tarzan,' said Tim.

'Why do a project about Tarzan?' said Andrew.

'Tarzan's easy,' said Tim. 'You just cut him out and stick him in.'

'Fish are easier,' said Victor.

'Why not do worms then?' said Andrew. 'Nothing could be easier than worms. Wiggle-wiggle-wiggle: all over in a second. Page one, worms are long and thin. Page two, worms are round.'

Victor began to grin but Tim sat down to give the idea serious consideration. Victor's grin became wider, revealing teeth like Stonehenge.

'I reckon you're catching on,' he said. 'Why don't you do worms?'

'I want to do something interesting,' said Andrew.

'Ho,' said Victor. 'You'll come to a bad end, you will.'

They went round the room. Andrew noticed that nearly all the boys were doing a project on fish or fishing. The girls tended to specialize in horses except for Jeanette Butler, who wouldn't let them see hers.

'Why don't you go and stand in the road and catch cars?' said Jeanette, giving them a hefty shove when they tried to look.

'Give us a kiss,' said Victor and got a poke in the chest instead.

'I think I'll do motor racing,' said Andrew when they got back to Victor's desk. 'I know a bit about that, already. Me and my Dad used to go to Brand's Hatch a lot, when we lived in Kent.'

APPENDIX VI: 'The Year the Schools Began Teaching the Telephone Directory' by *Merrill Harmin and Sidney B. Simon*

No one quite knew what had been the motivating factor. It seemed unlikely that the Council for Basic Education was behind it. Sputnik itself seemed a long way off. Some harsh critics, seeking a scapegoat, suspected the Telephone Company, but upon closer examination it was clear that they might have had as much to lose as they would to gain.

No, it was the superintendent's decision, and no apparent pressure group seemed to have motivated it. The memorandum went out on March 18th. It was simple and to the point.

> Beginning with the Fall term, all 7th. grade classes will be held responsible for learning the contents of our local telephone directory. Each teacher, working in cooperation with his or her immediate supervisor, will evolve the methods and procedures necessary to effect an efficient and appropriate achievement of the above-stated goal.

You can imagine the buzzing that went on in the men's faculty room. Some said that the memo was a first step towards a merit pay plan. Others were convinced that it had something to do with Admiral Rickover. An intellectual blamed it on that 'Bruner guy'. In the women teachers' room there was a more sedate but none the less bitter inquiry. 'Just what is the old boy up to now?' 'Do you think there will be a system-wide test?' 'I wonder if any company has brought out review books yet?'

Labor Day with its sad, fond farewell to the summer came and went. School was off and roaring. Most of the teachers weren't settled enough to give the students the telephone directories until the second day of class, but out they came and then it began, usually with some motivation such as this: 'Boys and girls. We are going to have an exciting new unit this term. As a way of studying our city, we're going through this amazing collection of information which tells us about the melting pot our city has been.' One teacher said, 'There will be an examination on this material in February, so you'd better learn it.'

Another approached it with, 'You wouldn't want to hurt my feelings by not memorizing these few names and numbers, would you children?'

Students dutifully received their directories, wrote their names on the

178

labels, and tactfully checked off the condition, 'new'. Feeling deeply his professional responsibilities, almost every teacher reminded his class that the books would be rechecked in February to see that no pages had been written upon or in any other way disfigured.

Miss Clark, a not atypical telephone directory teacher, was heard to say: 'Now boys and girls, let us look over our new textbooks. You will notice that it has a logical organization: it is arranged by the alphabet, as it were, and that's why they don't have a table of contents or an index. Although there are no illustrations in the part of the book we will be concerned with, you can always turn to the yellow pages for a picture or two. I've always enjoyed the listing for exterminators and moving vans. How about you?'

The students were quickly caught up in the enthusiasm the teachers projected and they pounced fiercely upon the new textbooks. Many looked at their teachers with new respect and admiration, for indeed the textbooks were arranged by the alphabet. Ah, to have education and wisdom. It was then that Miss Clark wrote on the board, in clear, Palmer-method letters: 'Tonight's assignment. Read and memorize the A's.'

Most of the students dragged home the telephone directories and after a short scrap with mothers about the TV-watching policy of the new term, they sat down to the evening's work. Read and memorize the A's. It was hard going, but this was not an easy world. Teachers, parents and students agreed that school needed to be more rigorous. Nothing comes easily, the students had been told, year after year. So they read and they memorized.

Morning came and the 7th. graders filed into their respective classes. 'Good morning, boys and girls,' greeted our typical telephone directory teacher. 'Did you do your homework last night?' (Not wishing to dampen the ardor of learning, she decided against a surprise quiz on this, the first morning of the unit. After all, an understanding of early adolescent behaviour had been part of her background.)

'All right, students, let's begin. What is Gregory Arnold's phone number?' A hush fell over the room, but almost instantly, three hands shot up.

'Eloise,' the teacher said.

Eloise answered, her voice more questioning than answering, 'Tr 8-9754.'

'Very good, Eloise,' the teacher said, 'but please, class, let's use the fullname of the exchange. Digital dialing is not completely with us yet. Let's say, Triumph 8-9754. Next, class, tell us who lives at 174 N, Maple Street.' Almost all of the hands went up. The teacher smiled benevolently. She had asked them an easy one, thrown out to give everyone a little feeling of success. It was the address of Mr Appleby, the principal, and almost everyone knew about the old mansion he lived in. The teacher, always striving to provide for individual differences, called on the slowest learner in the class and he gave the right answer. Everyone felt warm and good, 'Now boys and girls, we'll take up a little more difficult topic. Whose number is Wentworth 4-7312?' Panic spread through the class. No one seemed to know. Could she have slipped in a number from the B's? Finally, after the silence seemed unbearable, one hand, timidly, climbed towards the ceiling.

'Yes, Henry?' the teacher asked.

'I'm not sure, Miss Clark, but is it Frank Abelard?'

'Now, Henry, I'm asking the questions. Do you know or don't you? Do you wish us to count "Frank Abelard" as your answer?'

Was she supporting now, giving a hint that Frank Abelard was, indeed, the correct answer? Henry wasn't sure. It was difficult to figure Miss Clark sometimes.

'Well', he said, 'I guess I'm not sure.'

'But Henry', she said, 'you were right! It was Frank Abelard. You must have more confidence in yourself. Confidence is the substance of maturity. Right? Now, the next question. What is the name of the home appliance repair company on Front Street?' One hand went up instantly and the teacher was taken a bit aback. 'Yes, Gloria, do you know the answer?'

'I certainly do. That's my father, Miss Clark.'

'That's all very nice, Gloria, but we're here to find out if you did the assignment or not, so I think I had better give you another question. What is the phone number of the American Bar Association?' A wave of laughter quickly spread through the group. Most of them knew, but Miss Clark didn't, that very often Gloria's father was not available to fix a reluctant washing machine because he just happened to be in a bar, albeit not usually the American one. Gloria didn't answer, she just blushed, and Miss Clark said, 'Now, Gloria, you'll just have to do your work more conscientiously. This is a difficult unit and I want our class to do well in the finals. You're just going to have to work harder, Gloria, and that goes for the rest of you as well.'

The hand of a boy named Edward went up from the back row. 'Miss Clark, can I ask you a question?' 'Now, now, Edward,' Miss Clark said, 'Time is running out and we have all of those A's to cover over this period. Please save your question. Later, perhaps, in February, we can take it up. Back to our work, class. Which big industrial company in our town has two phone numbers?'

And so it went. Through the B's and through the C's. The students (many of them) studied and the teachers (all of them) cross-examined. After the D's there was increasing anxiety in the air as teachers began to have quizzes. But everyone seemed to know that it was the big marking-period test which was to count the most. That was the time for nerves! Miss Clark was one teacher who did place equal emphasis upon quizzes and tests, and so, of course, anxiety in her room was at a more constant level.

Many questions were raised in the school and in the community about this new seventh-grade curriculum. It wasn't long, however, before a united front of teachers, principals, and the superintendent worked out, in more or less trial-and-error fashion, a set of answers that became quite standard. Soon no one bothered to ask the questions any longer, for the answers had become predictable. For the historically-minded, here is a sample of the more pesky questions.

Q. Why learn the telephone book?
A. It develops good study habits which will be necessary in college and it trains the student to concentrate and apply himself, qualities which are useful in adult life. Among other things, disciplined adults are what we want.
Q. Won't they just forget the information after the tests?
A. The less bright student will most likely forget a lot. However, we intend to have regular reviews in later grades and consequently the retention curve will hold fairly satisfactorily.
Q. Why work so hard learning the telephone book when the directories are so handy when you actually need one?
A. After all, this could be said about any subject we teach. If we want our people to look up information when they need it, why teach anything? Furthermore, life is hard and the sooner our students learn this the better off they will be.

There were, of course, some students who did not concentrate enough to learn the phone book. It is not easy to run a school. There are slow learners in every community. These students were identified and plans were made to place them in special remedial classes the following term, classes which would work mainly on the yellow pages. The color, illustration, greater interest value, and reduced amount of material were expected to result in success for all but the fundamentally bad or lazy. Some children, it was readily acknowledged, just wouldn't learn no matter what a school did.

Back in the classrooms it was letter after letter until the word was out that there would be a system-wide mid-term examination on A through M. Oh, the cram sessions which were organized by eager mothers, the with-held allowances which were used as bludgeons, the diligent studying which went on! Never before did so many telephone numbers, addresses, and names get committed to so many memories.

Some boy students in the group spent their hours making small strips of answers which they taped to their shins and which were read later by slowly lifting their trouser legs.

Some girls wrote their answers upon flat throat lozenges. A few did nothing; they were non-motivated and didn't seem to care to become other than non-motivated. The only numbers they could get even a little excited about were the ones they phoned regularly themselves.

On the day of the test there were the usual amount of absences due to nervous stomachs. The teachers grudgingly set aside time for make-up exams, vowing to make them harder than the regular exams, 'otherwise, everyone will want to wait for the make-up test.' So the test was given, the papers marked, the grades carefully recorded in the appropriate grade books, and the teaching routine resumed.

But Miss Clark became increasingly uneasy. She was getting weary of asking, 'Who lives at so-and-so? Whose number is such-and-such?' Dull days. Slowly the rich memories of her undergraduate days in education courses came back. She sifted through the jargon and searched for ideas. . . .

The next Monday it was a new Miss Clark. The change rippled through the rows with electrifying results. Miss Clark had gone 'progressive'. For one thing, she organized a field trip. She and her class went off on a long walk to look up some of the houses in the 'N's'. It was difficult to plan, but Miss Clark felt that at least she was doing something worthwhile. Then she came up with the idea of inviting a guest speaker to come to class to talk about the P's. She obtained a film strip on the R's, but it turned out to be about the 'Three R's' and she couldn't use it. She attempted to organize committee work on the T's but the committee could find nothing to do, she had to scrap that idea. Miss Clark programmed the U's and this helped some. They had a bulletin board display on the V's – 'Victory Lunch and Veteran's Taxi Cab Service'. She did role playing on the W's, had a discussion-debate on the X's and then, with that handsome Mr Brown in Room 107, she did team teaching on the Y's.

By the time the Z's were reached, she was worrying about transfer of training. Would they really know how to use their knowledge? And, then, she had had no 'correlated motor behaviour training,' as they sometimes called it in college. So Miss Clark's class spent two whole days, courtesy of the public relations department of the phone company, practicing dialing the numbers they had learned (on eighteen telephones of various colors and shapes). It was noisy, and difficult to supervise, even though the students were carefully grouped, sociometrically, but Miss Clark was willing to risk a little to be a good teacher.

Finally, this too had to end. The final exam was a mere six weeks away. So, in Miss Clark's class, as well as in all the others, thirty days were spent in review for the 'Big Test'.

Review was no fun for anyone. The first week of June came with the sweetness of summer air. The girls in their barearmed summer dresses flitted in and out of the classrooms while the boys seemed slower than ever. Finally, the test was taken, the papers marked, and the term was over. A sense of heavy relief settled upon Miss Clark and all the others. The teachers gathered in the telephone directories, properly disciplined those who had written in their books, and stacked the directories in piles of eager readiness. September was not far away.

Miss Clark felt strangely tired. It wasn't that she had really worked harder this term. The feeling of being drained came from something else. Exactly what she wasn't sure and as she walked to her mailbox she was pondering this problem. There was a blue slip of paper in her mailbox amongst the more routine notices. It was a memo from the superintendent.

> The success of the telephone directory project initiated by this office has earned the well-deserved respect and admiration of the entire community. The rigorous efforts you and your students have made have not gone unnoticed. Certain thoughtful groups of concerned citizens within our district have urged this office to give this project the nation-wide publicity it deserves and also to move the content down further into the elementary schools. We agree with those critics who say that we are long overdue in our efforts to reform the softness of the elementary curriculum.
>
> Consequently, we are assigning to the 5th. grade the community's telephone directory. Out of appreciation to those faculty members among our 7th. grade who gave so much to our pioneer efforts in this content area, we are assigning 7th. grade teachers the exciting task of teaching the telephone directory of our State Capitol. The 6th. grades, to make the study complete, will combine their study of French with at least one unit on various sections of the Paris, France, telephone directory. This is dependent on whether or not we can obtain government or foundation assistance to purchase the suitable directories, however. You will hear more in September. Have a most pleasant summer.

The blue sheet slipped from Miss Clark's hand and floated to the floor but she seemed not to notice.

APPENDIX VIII: 'Arithmetic' by *Carl Sandburg*

Arithmetic is where numbers fly like pigeons in and out of your head.
Arithmetic tells you how many you lose or win if you know how many you had before you lost or won.
Arithmetic is seven eleven all good children go to heaven – or five six bundle of sticks.
Arithmetic is numbers you squeeze from your head to your hand to your pencil to your paper till you get the answer
Arithmetic is where the answer is right and everything is nice and you can look out of the window and see the blue sky – or the answer is wrong and you have to start all over again and try again and see if it comes out this time.
If you take a number and double it and double it again and then double it a few more times, the number gets bigger and bigger and goes higher and higher and only arithmetic can tell you what the number is when you decide to quit doubling.
Arithmetic is where you have to multiply – and you carry the multiplication table in your head and hope you won't lose it.
If you have two animal crackers, one good and one bad, and you eat one and a striped zebra with streaks all over him eats the other, how many animal crackers will you have if somebody offers you five six seven and you say No no no and you say Nay nay nay and you say Nix nix nix?
If you ask your mother for one fried egg for breakfast and she gives you two fried eggs and you eat both of them, who is better in arithmetic, you or your mother?

APPENDIX IX: Games Educators Play by *David Johnson*, Senior Primary Adviser, Manchester

1. *I Remember When* This is a typical game played by old-timers in the field. No matter what the idea may be to effect change, they are always ready to knock it down by proclaiming there is nothing new about the idea. It is something which occurred 20 or 30 years ago and was unsuccessful then, so why bother with it now? This type of game is most pronounced in a stable staff of individuals who have 'died on the vine' in their jobs.

2. *Smoke Screens* This type of game consists primarily of diversionary manoeuvres by an adept individual who subtly throws out smoke screens of seemingly related but actually unrelated topics which confuse the issue. He or she confuses everyone in the group until the idea becomes lost or bogged down and the group decides it is not worth pursuing any further.

3. *If Only I Had Time* This is a typical rationalization, so an individual or a staff does not even have to become concerned with considering change at all. This excuse of If Only I Had Time can, in some cases, be very realistic, but for many it is their game. When you analyse this game, you find the type of person who uses it is absorbed in minutiae and activities of low priority which do keep him or her busy and provide a seemingly logical excuse for him or her to use.

4. *The Poor Teachers and Children* The person who plays this game is adept at using a maudling, sentimental attitude. He or she proclaims teachers and children are confronted with so many things – what are we trying to do to them now? Who wants to be the dirty dog who hurts teachers and children?

5. *He/She Means Well, But* The technique here is that the one who proposes change means well but doesn't really understand things. This is also a typical response of the 'experienced' to the young educator. It is a beautiful technique to negate the proposal in a seemingly pleasant manner.

6. *Now I've Got You* This is the game which can be played by someone who has a great deal of sophistication. Typically, he or she will allow the idea of change to progress along to a certain point where he or she will then come out with a 'sword of Damocles' through statements such as, 'Well, you know what research says about this', or 'You know that so-and-so, an authority in the field, feels this way about this type of idea', etc. In this game a proposer of change is led down the primrose path until the sword falls on his or her neck.

186

7. *It's All Mine* This game is played by the kind of person whose ideas are solely his or her own, and they won't let anyone become involved with them either to assist or even to offer suggestions or criticisms. This person becomes so all-possessive about their ideas that it is impossible for them to implement them.

8. *If It Weren't for Them* This is related to game no. 3 (*If Only I Had Time*) in that the blame is placed upon someone else for change not occurring. This allows a person never to be at fault himself or herself and they can blame situations such as lack of working facilities, no time for pursuing ideas, poor salaries, on others' ineptness for preventing him or her from initiating change.

APPENDIX X: Confronting Avoidance

The following strategies are from a range proposed by Phillips and Fraser (1982). They represent suggested starting points for developing your own thoughts in this area.

Example of avoidance or denial in action	Strategy being used by the person	Possible way of confronting it
Person uses general-isations as a basis for believing that he/she cannot do anything differently 'After all that is the way the system is and everyone has to learn to cope as best they can'.	Generalising	'How specifically does this relate to the children that you actually teach?' 'Do you really feel that powerless?'
Person uses a catastrophic fantasy as an excuse for avoiding responsibility and not taking action 'I couldn't possibly do that, my colleagues would never speak to me again'.	Creating catastrophies	'Would it have to end up that way?' 'What is the worst thing that could happen to you?'
Person talks about anything and every-thing rather than face up to his/her particular problem. 'It's funny how	Rambling	'How does this relate to what we are discussing?' 'You still haven't answered my ques-tion'.

things happen, I went to see David the other day and he was telling me . . .'		*Focus* on 'what' and 'how' rather than 'why'.
Person blocks out awareness of any internal dialogue between an experience and his/her own feelings and thoughts. 'That doesn't worry me at all'	Creating internal blocks	'Not the slightest bit?' 'What are you feeling?' 'That doesn't seem to match your non-verbal messages'
Person blocks out awareness of other people's behaviour and attitudes 'I don't think that children worry about tests' (child is on the verge of tears)	Creating external blocks	'Have a look at ——, What do you see?' 'What are you aware of?'
Person minimises his/ her own feelings or the extent of his/her problems as the basis for believing that they don't have to be faced 'It doesn't matter, honestly, it is not really worth worry- ing about'.	Minimising	'Does it really not matter? You obviously thought it worth talking about'. 'Even if it isn't important, tell me any feelings you have about it'.
Person has rigid expectations of others and frequently uses them as a basis for subsequently being angry or disappointed	Creating rigid expectations of others	'How long have you come to have this expectation?' 'What are the consequences for you of having this expectation?'

'After all I've done for this school I expect better treatment than this'.		
Person uses old rules of behaviour even though they are not helpful in dealing with current problems and relationships 'We've never done that sort of thing in this school'.	Sticking to obsolete rules	'That sounds like a rule for you' 'How does that rule help in this situation?'

APPENDIX XI: 'The Three Year Itch' by *Angela Anning*

I used to wonder why so many of the 'successful' primary headteachers I knew took to one of several clearly defined courses three or four years into their headships. One course turned sharply sideways, taking the headteacher to another school, a decision rationalized as a desire for a new challenge. Another course began to slope downwards into complacency – slowly at first, but the gradient soon became steeper. A third veered away from schools altogether into the rarefied atmosphere of the advisory service, union politics or teacher training. The illusion was of an upwards slope, but in effect the track soon appeared to bog them down in muddy fields of bureaucracy.

Three years into my first headship, I understand what happens. The truth is that a headteacher can manage the superficial revamping of a school if he or she is sharp enough to define priorities at an early stage and pace the instigation of changes so that staff, children and the head's own health remain intact.

The race is run something like this. The environment is the first priority for changes – corridors are cleared of unsightly old furniture; next, and more daringly, the classrooms get the same treatment; tubs of flowers for the entrance hall are hired from the local parks department; cloakrooms are stripped of ancient coat hooks and transformed into libraries, craft areas, resource banks.

Ancient textbooks and the contents of store cupboards – birds' nests, shells, oil-cloth maps of the British Empire, a thousand lined exercise books with musty yellow pages and all the paraphernalia reflecting your predecessor's siege mentality – all those are ruthlessly spirited away in black bags during half-term holidays when tetchy members of staff are not around to protest.

Meanwhile, curriculum guidelines are drawn up at endless staff meetings, the emphasis swinging wildly according to the strengths of the headteacher and staff and pressures from local authority which is, in turn, under pressure from DES directives, and applied by the hapless advisory staff. The staff are 'democratically' involved in changes, even when they protest, because all the management and in-service courses tell us that this is the only way to effective change.

Willing and unwilling staff are despatched to observe good practice in other schools and coerced into attending workshops and courses and into experimenting with new resources. The parents are invited to evening meetings to approve changes already firmly instigated by the headteacher and staff in hollow gestures of consultation. Governing bodies too are informed retrospectively of fundamental changes in curriculum policy: a paragraph buried among the complaints about leaking roofs and broken boundary railings in the headteacher's report. It is all beginning to look pretty good.

The illusion is that at some point you will reach a finishing line and triumph. But three years on, the real rather than the presenting problems loom large ahead and you suddenly realize that the Beecher's Brook of effecting change in the school is the area about which management courses tell you little or nothing – that is making real, rather than superficial, changes in classroom practice.

It is a desperate and dangerous leap to make. It requires the headteacher and the staff of a school to take risks and place enormous trust in each other. The disquieting findings from classroom-based research about the gap between the teacher's perception of what is happening in the classroom and the empirical evidence about what is really happening make depressing reading.

The headteacher, observing classrooms throughout the school, acknow-ledges, if only privately, that the same thing is happening there.

Rather than sit back and wait passively for the next brickbat, teachers must be encouraged to study their own and colleagues' classrooms and think about how to improve inadequate practice. But it is at this crucial point that many headteachers lose their nerve, drop the reins and dismount.

Yet descriptions of techniques for classroom observation and evaluation are readily available in current publications. The Open University 'Curriculum in Action' packs provide excellent starting points. At least four university departments actively encourage and support teachers who want to work alongside researchers in evaluating school practice – Leicester, East Anglia, Lancaster and the Cambridge Institute. The hardware for collecting data – tape recorders, cameras and video-cameras – has never been easier for the non-technically minded to operate.

So since information, support and equipment are not the stumbling blocks, why do so many headteachers baulk at this point? The truth is that the kinds of issues raised by careful observations of classroom practice are not comfortable. They are likely to challenge many assumptions about the teaching and learning process. How can we deal with the time 'wasted' by many children in the school day? How can we increase their motivation? How can children be encouraged to function effectively in cooperative group tasks? How can we resolve the conflict between the needs of the individual child and the needs of the class or group? How can the teacher organize teaching time most effectively? How can the quality of teacher-pupil and pupil-pupil interactions be improved?

Confronting such classroom-based issues forces a thinking school to look beyond the cosmetic changes in the school environment, resources and content-based curriculum.

The process has to involve genuine self-evaluation. In contrast, the l.e.a. documents for self-evaluation are a contradiction in terms. The list of questions to which schools are required to respond, although sweetened with the occasional open-ended question, are heavily loaded and suggest a prescribed norm or ideal against which the school is expected to measure its own practice. Schools should now be in a position to move on and define their own areas of concern. Analysis of their observations of classroom practice should help to clarify these needs and hopefully cut through the kind of educational jargon that is often a substitute for action in schools.

The researchers and theorists may provide the context for educational changes but the staff and headteacher are uniquely able to define and implement them. My guess is that it is the dawning realization of this challenge and its attendant responsibility that sends those bright young colleagues of mine galloping off at a tangent.

APPENDIX XII: 'A Fuzzytale' by *Claude M. Steiner*

Once upon a time, a long time ago, there lived two very happy people called Tim and Maggie with two children called John and Lucy. To understand how happy they were, you have to understand how things were in those days. You see, in those happy days everyone was given at birth a small, soft, Fuzzy Bag. Any time a person reached into this bag he was able to pull out a Warm Fuzzy. Warm Fuzzies were very much in demand because whenever somebody was given a Warm Fuzzy it made him feel warm and fuzzy all over. People who didn't get Warm Fuzzies regularly were in danger of developing a sickness in their backs which caused them to shrivel up and die.

In those days it was very easy to get Warm Fuzzies. Any time that somebody felt like it, he might walk up to you and say, 'I'd like to have a Warm Fuzzy.' You would then reach into your bag and pull out a Fuzzy the size of the little girl's hand. As soon as the Fuzzy saw the light of day it would smile and blossom into a large, shaggy Warm Fuzzy. You then would lay it on the person's shoulder or head or lap and it would snuggle up and melt right against their skin and make them feel good all over.

People were always asking each other for Warm Fuzzies, and since they were always given freely, getting enough of them was never a problem. There was always plenty to go around and as a consequence everyone was happy and felt warm and fuzzy most of the time.

One day a bad witch became angry because everyone was so happy and no one was buying her potions and salves. The witch was very clever and she devised a very wicked plan. One beautiful morning she crept up to Tim while Maggie was playing with their daughter and whispered in his ear, 'See here, Tim, look at all the Fuzzies that Maggie is giving to Lucy: You know, if she keeps it up, eventually she is going to run out and then there won't be any left for you.'

Tim was astonished. He turned to the witch and said 'Do you mean to tell me that there isn't a Warm Fuzzy in our bag every time we reach into it?'

And the witch said, 'No, absolutely not, and once you run out, that's it. You don't have any more.' With this, she flew away on her broom, laughing and cackling hysterically.

Tim took this to heart and began to notice every time Maggie gave up a Warm Fuzzy to someone else. Eventually he got very worried and upset because he liked Maggie's Warm Fuzzies very much and did not want to give them up. He certainly did not think it was right for Maggie to be spending all her Warm Fuzzies on the children and on other people. He began to complain every time he saw Maggie giving a Warm Fuzzy to somebody else, and because Maggie liked him very much, she stopped giving Warm Fuzzies to other people as often, and reserved them for him.

The children watched this and soon began to get the idea that it was wrong to give up Warm Fuzzies any time you were asked or felt like it. They would watch their parents closely and whenever they felt that one of their parents was giving too many Fuzzies to others, they also began to object. They began to feel worried whenever they gave away too many Warm Fuzzies. Even though they found a Warm Fuzzy every time they reached into their bag, they reached in less and less and became more stingy. Soon people began to notice the lack of Warm Fuzzies, and they began to feel less and less fuzzy.

They began to shrivel up and occasionally, people would die from lack of Warm Fuzzies. More and more people went to the witch to buy her potions and salves even though they didn't seem to work.

Well, the situation was getting very serious indeed. The bad witch, who had been watching all of this, didn't really want the people to die, so she devised a new plan. She gave everyone a bag that was very similar to the Fuzzy Bag except that this one was cold while the Fuzzy Bag was warm. Inside of the witch's bag were Cold Pricklies. Cold Pricklies did not make people feel warm and fuzzy, but made them feel cold and prickly instead. But, they did prevent people's backs from shriveling up. So, from then on, every time somebody said, 'I want a Warm Fuzzy,' people who were worried about depleting their supply would say, 'I can't give you a Warm Fuzzy, but would you like a Cold Prickly?' Sometimes two people would walk up to each other, thinking they could get a Warm Fuzzy, but one or the other of them would change his mind and they would wind up giving each other Cold Pricklies. So, the end result was that while very few people were dying, a lot of people were still unhappy and feeling very cold and prickly.

The situation got very complicated because, since the coming of the witch, there were less and less Warm Fuzzies around, so Warm Fuzzies, which used to be thought of as free as air, became extremely valuable. This caused people to do all sorts of things in order to obtain them.

Before the witch had appeared, people used to gather in groups of three or four or five, never caring who was giving Warm Fuzzies to whom. After the coming of the witch, people began to pair off and to reserve all their Warm Fuzzies for each other exclusively. If ever one of the two persons forgot himself and gave a Warm Fuzzy to someone else, he would immediately feel guilty about it because he knew his partner would probably resent the loss of a Warm Fuzzy. People who could not find a generous partner had to buy their Warm Fuzzies and had to work long hours to earn the money. Another thing which happened was that some people would take Cold Pricklies – which were limitless and freely available – coat them white and fuzzy and pass them on as Warm Fuzzies. These counterfeit Warm Fuzzies were really Plastic Fuzzies, and they caused additional difficulties. For instance, two people would get together and freely exchange Plastic Fuzzies, which presumably should make them feel good, but they came away feeling bad instead. Since they thought they had been exchanging Warm Fuzzies, people grew very confused about this, never realizing that their cold prickly feelings were really the result of the fact that they had been given a lot of Plastic Fuzzies.

So, the situation was very, very dismal and it all started because of the coming of the witch who made people believe that someday, when least expected, they might reach into their Warm Fuzzy Bag and find no more.

Not long ago a young woman with big hips, born under the sign of Aquarius, came to this unhappy land. She had not heard about the bad witch and was not worried about running out of Warm Fuzzies. She gave them out freely, even when not asked. They called her the Hip Woman and disapproved of her because she was giving the children the idea that they should not worry about running out of Warm Fuzzies. The children liked her very much because they felt good around her and they, too, began to give out Warm Fuzzies whenever they felt like it. The grown-ups became concerned and decided to pass a law to protect the children from depleting their supplies of Warm Fuzzies. The law made it a criminal offence to give out Warm Fuzzies in a reckless manner. The children, however, seemed not to care and in spite of the law, they continued to give each other Warm Fuzzies whenever they felt like it and always when asked. Because there were many, many children, almost as many as grown-ups, it began to look as if maybe they would have their way.

As of now it is hard to say what will happen. Will the grown-up forces of law and order stop the recklessness of the children? Are the grown-ups going to join with the Hip Woman and the children in taking a chance that there will always be as many Warm Fuzzies as needed? Will they remember the days their children are trying to bring back when Warm Fuzzies were abundant because people gave them away freely?

BIBLIOGRAPHY

Anning, A. (1983) 'The Three Year Itch', *The Times Educational Supplement*, 24 June 1983

Bennis, W. and Shepard, H. (1956) 'A Theory of Group Development', *Human Relations*, *9*, 415-37

Chaplin, C. (1973) *My Autobiography*, Penguin, Harmondsworth

Cooley, C.H. (1964) *Human Nature and Social Order*, Scribner, New York

Georgiades, N.J. and Phillimore, L. (1975) 'The Myth of the Hero-innovator and Alternative Strategies for Organisational Change' in C.C. Keirnan and F.P. Woodford (eds), *Behaviour Modification with the Severely Retarded*, Elsevier Excerpta Medica, North Holland, pp. 313-19

Harmin, M. and Simon S.B. (1965) 'The Year the Schools Began Teaching the Telephone Directory', *Harvard Education Review*, *35*, 326-31

Janis, I. (1977) *Decision Making: a Psychological Analysis of Conflict, Choice and Commitment*, Free Press, New York

Laing, R.D. (1970) *Knots*, Tavistock, London

Mark, J. (1978) *Thunder and Lightnings*, Puffin, Harmondsworth

Merrit, J. *et al.* (1980) *Curriculum in Action: an Approach to Evaluation*, Open University Press, Milton Keynes

Mezirow, J. (1977) 'Perspective Transformation', *Studies in Adult Education*, *9*, 153-64

Peddiwell, J.A. (1939) *The Saber-tooth Curriculum*, McGraw-Hill, New York and London, pp. 24-44

Phillips, K. and Fraser, T. (1982) *The Management of Interpersonal Skills Training*, Gower, Aldershot

Rudduck, J. (1981) *Making the Most of the Short In-service Course*, Schools Council Working Paper 71, Methuen Educational, London

Sandburg, C. (1950) *Complete Poems*, Rupert Hart Davis

Shostak, G. (1982) 'Study 2: Teachers Visit other Schools' in J. Rudduck (ed.), *Teachers in Partnership: Four Studies of In-service Collaboration*, Longman for Schools Council, York, pp. 27-42

Steiner, C. (1974) *Scripts People Live: Transactional Analysis of Life*, Grove Press, New York

Tuckman, B. and Jensen, M. (1977) 'Stages of Small Group Development Revisited', *Group and Organisation Studies*, *2*,(4), 419-27

Warwick, D. (1982) *Running Effective Meetings*, Education for Industrial Society, London